NIRVANA AND ENERGY

The Truth Behind All Life

NIRVANA AND ENERGY

The Truth Behind All Life

Tammie Truong

NIRVANA AND ENERGY

The Truth Behind All Life

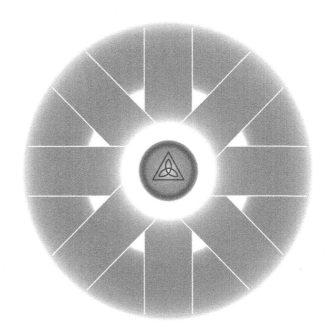

Keys to Mastery
Discover Ultimate Life Purpose and Fulfillment

ABOUT THE AUTHOR

Tammie is a Best Selling Author. Her first book: Chân Lý Và Năng Lượng was published Easter Day, 2020. Within three months Tammie became the best-selling author of spirituality books in Vietnam.

Her two day meditation courses started May 2020 and already there is a long waiting list. Everyone participating comes away with a greater sense of joy and enthusiasm to continue their personal inner journey toward Nirvana/The Zero Point. Former students gather to share the miracles they have experienced since the course and reveal how it has positively changed their life and that of their family toward freedom, joy, happiness, wellbeing, and even enlightenment.

People from 9 to 77 years old have joined Tammie's courses and been healed body, mind, and soul and realized Nirvana. Those who she has touched have found greater happiness, wellbeing, and freedom. Records are available on her YouTube channel and can be translated to share with the world.

People have been healed from ailments such as covid-19, prostate cancer and diabetes. One person who suffered insomnia for more than 20 years confirmed that after listening only once to Tammie's channel was able to sleep normally. That person then came to the course with her husband and both came away happily, free from all aches and pains. The wife can even see the world with the third eye.

Everyone that has come to Tammie's course is given a glimps of Nirvana. They start to experience greater intuition, discovering their uniqueness and special abilities. Some can even see celestial beings, pasts and futures (Akashic records), and different dimensions of reality by simply discovering their true nature - who they are at the core.

Tammie's unique power to heal is even accessed by those who connect with her through her YouTube channel. Many people are healed from low self-esteem/depression. Some can see the higher self of Tammie appearing in dreams to heal them. They wake up completely healed. They share these stories on her channel.

May all beings realize true freedom, true happiness, and experience a life of universal joy, love, and bliss.

I love you. You are amazing. Thank you.

Words are not the best tools to communicate Tammie's amazing abilities. She invites you to come to her two day meditation course and experience it yourself. It is free of charge. Donations received during and after the course from those who have felt the benefits are used to support future courses. Many old students who have experienced transformations refer family members and loved ones to her. Come and see for yourself. May this book alone bring healing, activate the flow of universal energy, and reveal the Nirvana that is within you. It is timeless, nameless, the zero point. It is your untouched dimension. And because it is untouched, it is your ultimate freedom. Once you have IT you can be happy and experience unconditional love. Only when you have happiness, freedom, and love that is beyond conditions can your life be truly fulfilled. I am experiencing that life right now and so are my students. May all of you in this very life be healed body, mind & soul, realizing your true freedom/true nature/Nirvana.

Tammie Truong

GRATITUDE

I wish to express my deepest love and gratitude to all life forms especially my near and dear masters, parents, relatives, friends and all beings whom I directly or indirectly come into contact with. Without your participation, this beautiful journey would not be possible.

This realization has allowed me to enjoy my existence to the fullest and live my true purpose. The sense of fulfillment just gets more and more beautiful along this path of alignment with the Source that I am and that you are.

Source is the origin of all there is. This infinite dimension holds the key to the highest creations of mastery, wisdom, joy, and happiness. This path has been sought by the highest intelligent beings of all time. Since ancient times many have realized it because it is the origin of who we are before we were born and who we return when we die. Many beings who discovered this truth refer to this unnamable energy as Source, Nirvana, God, Christ Consciousness, Buddha Consciousness, etc. Indeed, these terms point to the same thing: the Truth. Only the truth sets us free by becoming one with universal intelligence and infinite freedom. The Truth is always available within each and every one of us because it is who we really are, the limitless and sufferless dimension, giving clarity to all human experiences and decisions.

In this book, I use the terms Source, Nirvana, and Truth to point to the Unnamable. Language itself is not the experience, it is only the pointer to truth, only direct experience of truth will set you free and it is the very intention of this book. May you realize your origin and experience the highest life purpose and fulfillment in this very life, my love.

Tammie Truong

CONTENTS

OPENING

Dear beloved, the journey that I am about to share with you has brought me increased clarity, joy, and fulfillment every day. This path to a happy life is available not just to selected individuals like Buddha, Jesus, or other gifted human beings, but to all mankind. The difference between individuals like Buddha, Jesus, and other beings who achieved enlightenment is that they realized the truth within through different paths such as meditation, yoga, and sudden realizations. From the perspective of Unity Consciousness these beings shared the truth to all others, for they knew that every one of us possesses the same truth and fulfillment within.

"I am the light of the world, whoever follows me will not walk in darkness, but will have the light of life." - Jesus

"Every man possesses the Buddha Nature (Or everyone can realize Nirvana, Enlightenment)" - Buddha

These declarations assert that every human being can access this path of clarity, true love, and happiness. In fact, many such as Yoga Nanda, Gandhi, Ramana Marhashi, Papaji, Mooji Papa, and Eckhart Tolle have realized the same truth and have shared it with the world. The way each enlightened One discovered the truth is completely different, however, the truth itself is only One: The Unnamable.

INTENTION SETTING

As everything starts with a thought or intention, the following might represent your reason for reading this book.

It is my intention to realize my true nature through this book, the Nirvana that I AM originally. Thus, I will consciously access and allow into my life: joy, happiness, and full mastery in every moment while I am in this body. As I live a conscious and happy life, at the time of departure, I will leave my body consciously and return to the infinite freedom dimension of Nirvana that I am.

ENERGY OF THE BOOK

Since this book flows from the now, the oneness energy, it is not for intellectualizing. When you really connect with the flow of energy beyond words or understanding, you connect with the power of the Source. This alignment will eradicate a limited belief system and activate intuition, flow (freedom), and wisdom. Just allowing the flow of energy when reading this book, you may feel lightness and subtle happiness but not be able to really understand the meaning. This means you have connected with the book at the deepest level. Those who are aligned or relaxed while reading will easily connect with my book in this dimension. This dimension is always better than the dimension of mental understanding and intellectualizing because nirvana is a direct experience of freedom, not the understanding of the words. This book easily gets you in the flow of connectedness to Source Intelligence for it came from that state itself.

THE PRIMORDIAL SOUND

Different traditions use different terms when referring to the Primordial Sound: Cosmic sound, OM sound, one hand clapping, etc. This is the purest form of sound, the purest vibration. It is ever present and those who have a calm mind can easily hear it. Once you connect with it, you can always hear it. Many call this the ringing in the ears... however, the more you hear this means the more you are in alignment with who you really are or your true nature.

This sound is the first child of Source. You are Source the moment you hear this sound, only Source is the dimension subtler than this. Your mind will try to interpret what this sound is. The mind is always trying to interpret past knowledge, either positive or negative. Once you align with equanimity or Source dimension, the more often you will see clearly how the mind functions. Only then you will be able to use it. That is when Mastery occurs.

MASTERY

The term Master is used for individuals who have mastered their mind. Only those who can master their mind can master their happiness, especially in today's world.

"A well tempted mind brings happiness" - Buddha

When we can't master our mind, we begin to lead our lives based on past memories which are very limiting. We make the same decisions, experience the same emotions, and come to the same conclusions based on those memories. This process of going around the same circle is called Karma.

When we change, everything will change for us. We must make sure we are changing for the better because whatever we generate, we attract. It is called cause & effect. When being happy is caused, the effect attracts more and more happiness.

Being miserable attracts more and more misery. The law of attraction is indeed 'cause & effect' itself.

In my very first 10 days of the Vipassana Meditation course, I experienced the dimension of oneness energy, experiencing everything as pure vibration, pure love - bliss and nothing else. Tears of joy ran down my cheeks for bliss was so intense that first time. This dimension/state is called Brahman in some traditions. It is pure unconditional love. There is an ultimate dimension after this: Nirvana. I experienced it two years later, with intense practice after the experience of Brahman consciousness. In this book, I want to present to you different paths to realize the same truth.

THE FORMLESS FORM

"*Energy cannot be created or destroyed, it can only be changed from one form to another.*" - Einstein

There are subatomic particles that govern the whole Cosmo including space itself. In other words, the space is formed by these subatomic particles that are formless to the mind's eye but visible to the eye of Source. This dimension exists at all times. Once you can see it, you can always see it. They are the particles that form our bodies, trees, animals, land, space, universes, multiverses, etc. Using quantum physics, my master helped me realize these particles when my mind was at the point of calm and alignment.

Years later, I discovered that these particles are called Rupa Kalapa in Theravada (Vipassana) Buddhist tradition. Other traditions call them God particles, formless form, energy, frequency, vibrations, etc. These are different names for the same thing. You will be able to see this as well. Anytime you see this, you are in perfect alignment with Source. Only Source is the dimension that is subtler than this. The mind might try to interpret or understand this dimension. It cannot be understood with the rational mind because this dimension is the subtlest reality of consciousness. Realization is direct experience, not conceptualizing.

THE RIGHT FOUNDATION

Before enlightenment people operate based on memory. Higher evolved beings operate based on higher frequencies of creativity, positivity, possibilities, etc. The nature of the mind fluctuates based on memories: good/bad, right/wrong, ugly/pretty, etc. All these dualities are based on past conclusions or belief systems. When not seen through the eyes of Source, human beings often distorted perception caused by their established belief system. That is why there are frequent arguments, disagreements, judgment, etc. They are all due to different filters of perception.

Building life and happiness on something that is so unstable does not seem wise. Like building a house on a stable foundation, building our life and happiness on something that is deathless and unchanging is a wise decision, isn't it? Nirvana or Source is the unchanging dimension of who we really are. Those who live aligned with this dimension can access universal wisdom with their clarity of mind. They are free from mental noises and are able to use the mind itself to serve their highest good as a creator. Only when we are happy and fulfilled, can we radiate that quality into the world.

THE ABSOLUTE

The Absolute is just another name for Source, Nirvana, or Truth. I experienced this during my two years as a nun in forest meditation centers in Myanmar and after Theravada Vipassana practice. My consciousness reached a state of perfect equanimity. I felt pure joy and bliss. The three factors that were critical to my reaching such a state were:

1. Enlightened, skillful masters.

2. A secluded, peaceful, loving, and supportive environment.

3. Intensive, continuous retreats in complete silence.

My body and mind were at the peak of bliss and lightness due to continued practice of mindfulness. One afternoon I experienced pure consciousness itself. It dissolved right before my very "eye". This "eye" is not the human eye but the eye of Source, beyond time-space and beyond consciousness itself. Absolute is the best word to describe this state. Only then I understood the Buddhist teachings about "Cessation of all Sufferings" to be true. The Absolute is the state beyond all suffering, the highest and ultimate freedom that the Sages of all time praise. It is a resting place of the realized ones.

However, there are two types of Nirvana. The Absolute Nirvana that I experienced through the path of purification (Theravada Vipassana) and Alive Nirvana which is often realized and taught by Zen masters and non-duality teachings. These two types of Nirvana are indeed supportive to each other to help us live a completely fulfilled life while connecting with the deathless dimension within.

TWO TYPES OF NIRVANA

1. ABSOLUTE NIRVANA

Nirvana is reached via a step by step purification path before the "Absolute" is realized. Let's discuss the pros and cons of this path.

Pros:

One directly experiences different states of consciousness through continuous intense practice in meditative environments and finally reaches Nirvana at the end of the path. The intense practice gives one the opportunity to dive deep inside to see the whole body/mind mechanism, how they are connected to one another, how they work and use continuous powerful mindfulness to purify old limited belief systems that bring suffering. One becomes more wholesome of thought, speech, and action on this path of purification. Again, energy cannot be created nor destroyed, it can simply be transformed. When we operate on a state of conscious awareness, this high frequency of pure consciousness will transform the energies of our old belief energy systems. Everything that arises in the body/mind will automatically be transformed by the state of conscious awareness. That is why this path is called the Path of Purification.

Cons:

It is step-by-step process and many have actually given up before enlightenment was reached because of one of the reasons below:

1. Not having the right environment for purification.

2. Not having the right guidance.

3. Not enough discipline or determination to realize the ultimate goal

4. Not having a correct balance between wisdom and faith. Not trusting one's own ability to attain enlightenment is very important because Nirvana is your very core being.

2. ALIVE NIRVANA

Alive Nirvana is taught in different traditions such as Zen and Non-dual teachings. Many teachers in our time like Eckhart Tolle, Adyashanti, Rupert Sprira, and Mooji Papa have shared what is at the core of all existence. This dimension is the absolute itself. Recognizing this dimension while being active in the world is to me most practical. Let's discuss pros and cons of this path.

Pros:

1. Often easy and immediate realization of our true nature with our Master's guidance.

2. Ability to live a life of true detachment. Spontaneous flow as Source. This formless state is itself a true state of allowance and fulfillment, key to mastery of the law of attraction.

3. Direct access to universal wisdom when allowing Source to operate through you. Tasting the increasing sweetness of freedom, happiness, and source intelligence along with one's life experience.

Cons:

1. Humans often only value something that is difficult to attain, thus doubt this formless dimension. In my case I no longer doubt Nirvana because I went through the systematic way to know that Nirvana is the best of the best. Before Nirvana, I experienced many states of bliss including seeing panic breath particles with both open and closed eyes. I also experienced the state of Brahman consciousness years prior to the experience of Nirvana.

2. This requires spiritual maturity to allow Source (the non-self state) to take charge of one's life. Without prior experience in the Path of Purification, the mind is often still to strong to allow the Source to take charge. Being near the wise masters and having sufficient trust at the earlier stages is necessary for advancement.

3. In the begining, the ego is often too strong to accept states beyond its

comprehension. Ego resists. It is easy to attach to something that is tangible but not to something that is intangible like Source.

In conclusion, this path allows ones true nature to guide life. This is truly "allowing God" to flow through us, the concept that enlightened Masters speak about.

Those who know, know who knows and who does not know. Those who don't know, do not know who knows and who does not know.

Those who know, will recognize this quote.

SOURCE INTELLIGENCE

The intelligence of life force can be seen all around us from trees, animals, earth, sun, cosmos, our body/mind, etc. The intelligence that sustains our life also effortlessly inhales and exhales life force or Prana/air to keep us oxygenated and alive. We always possess this intelligence. However, since every human being has it we rarely talk about this pure intelligence.

This pure intelligence is the heart of religion that all enlightened masters wanted to share with us. The common word that we use is wisdom. Those who are in unity with this pure intelligence are able to access the secret to human life and true happiness.

Since ancient times, those who realize the truth seem extraordinary in the human world. They seem to be joyful, content, happy, and have solutions to all life's problems.

Did you know that the difference between enlightened beings and the majority of humans today is the purity of mind? That is why enlightened people are also referred to as Saint/Sage. The only difference is that these beings turn inward to the internal guidance system/Source, the purity, the core of all existence.

As Source, they flow through life with ease and grace, automatically attracting the physical manifestations to support their wellbeing. They seem to attract with ease abundance, love, and greatness from the universe. Look at Mother Teresa for example. According to Abraham Hicks teaching, we are pure, positive energy sources. Our unconscious attachment to low frequencies or negative emotions are the very obstacles to abundance and fulfilled life itself.

LIFE PURPOSE AND FULFILLMENT

When one is in alignment, pure intelligence will know what to do at every moment. Let us observe the way our organs function. They always do their best. The liver never complains or is jealous of the heart though they are different. They all do their best to support life. When we skin our knee, the whole body intelligence works harmoniously to heal our skin without stress or confusion.

Through conscious awareness, one knows what one is good at, what makes one happy, what one is passionate about and what one is inspired to do. When you do what you love, challenges become your inspiration to expand to higher levels of creativity, joy, and fulfillment. That is how it works in my reality. I had never thought that I would become a writer or meditation teacher. Through alignment with Source, I synchronize with other aligned individuals. I resonate, take action, and realized my purpose. When we realize our true purpose, inspiration follows. The more I write, the more truth flows through me. I feel a deeper joy, greater, wisdom and connection with life. It fulfills my spirit. This path is fun beyond measure. The greater I am able to align my consciousness, the more proof I see in my life. Many others who are on the same path are drawn to me, they are the ones who also get to taste the joy being of service to others while doing what they love. We are all connected. I see so clearly that the more I serve others, the greater is my happiness and fulfillment. When I serve others, I serve myself.

UNCONDITIONAL LOVE OF PURE INTELLIGENCE

Universal intelligence has a quality of pure unconditional love. After directly experiencing different states of consciousness, I realized that during childhood I had already experienced these moments of truth from time to time but had no words for them. The experiences seem so real compared with all others I had in the world of duality, because at those precious moments I was more in alignment with who I really am. We can only forget what we are not, we cannot forget who we really are. Once you realize your true nature, you will recognize this.

One example is when I was about seven years old and sick. My grandma was taking care of me. I was laying in a hammock watching her making a special food for a sick, spoiled granddaughter to chew. Suddenly I had a flash of fresh purity that was beyond anything that I had experienced physically or mentally before. It was a very emotional, divine moment that I will always remember as if it just happened. I can recall it at any time. The experience of Nirvana/true Nature/Source can also be recalled anytime in ones consciousness after realization. This pure energy of love was beyond the physical bodies of my grandma and me. It is a bit different compared with Nirvana because pure love has a bit of pure divine taste to it while Nirvana is the state of Absolute. The more I allow Source to flow through me, the more frequently I experience these moments of pure love and bliss. This is the state of love beyond gender and beyond physical experience.

SEXUAL INTIMACY (TANTRA) AND ENLIGHTENMENT

Love is a state of inclusiveness where high frequency (good feeling) is prominent. Ego is thinking about, while love is at the level of being. Ego is about oneself versus others. Love is the state where the two agree to join together directly experiencing intimacy up to the peak of orgasm. I already passed through states of joy, bliss, tranquil, etc. prior to the experience of oneness and nirvana. I also experienced orgasm frequently in my intimate relationships. I know that orgasm itself is the state of bliss without having to meditate. Besides joy, bliss, and tranquility I also experienced cosmic consciousness at the point of orgasm. It was only then that I realized the teaching of Tantra were valid. In other words, love is a process of raising frequency beyond ego up to cosmic consciousness, the highest state of human experience. That is why many can't resist sexual intimacy. It means we can't resist uniting with the highest frequencies of who we really are. When this process of raising frequency is conscious, it is called Tantra.

Every human being can access the state of Nirvana or true nature on a daily basis without knowing it. It is called true nature because it is the very core of who we are. When we are most natural, we flow as "that". There is no time or space because it is beyond the thinking mind. Time-space appears when the thinking mind is involved. When we touch fire, our natural intelligence automatically moves the hand away without any thinking time. We always flow within that intelligence. Enlightenment is realizing that we are already rooted in this dimension of freedom and intelligence.

Orgasm is one of the direct ways of returning "home" to who we really are, the state of being, blissful, beyond thinking mind. That is the very reason every human being loves sexual intimacy.

The further we are from "home" the more we feel lost and ungrounded. In other words, the more we attach to the ego mind, the more suffering we experience because it is far from our natural pure positive state of being.

Harmony or unity in one sense is the state of perfect yin-yang balance. It is complete merging and dissolving of ego through the act of love or aligning with higher frequencies. Ego dissolves in bliss for bliss is a state of being while ego is the state of linear thinking. Yin-yang balance can give birth to a state of consciousness that is beyond gender. The super consciousness.

Along my journey of conscious alignment, I have been blessed to come into contact with high frequency beings that were aligned with my energetic frequency. Some traditions call these individuals soulmates or twin-flames. They exist in my experience.

TWIN-FLAME AND SOULMATE

My intimacy with my twin-flame was sacred. I was so peaceful in his energy field and he felt the same. In fact, I can always sense his energy field of light and love. Every time we think about each other we feel happy. We are each other's inspiration even when we are not physically together.

We met one another at the time I was at my peak of peace and alignment. This was after the first three months of meditation with the first Master. Note that twin-flame energy is universal energy. It normally happens when one partner has already reached the state of alignment and mastery and the other half is on the way to reaching the same state. In my case, my twin-flame was the one that attained higher enlightenment and I was close to his state of consciousness. That was how we attracted one another. It was the universal law of energy, the law of attraction.

When we first met, his body cells vibrated with immense ecstasy. He experienced love at first sight. It was so strong that it opened his heart to a higher level of love and joy for days. After we met, we constantly missed each other. For the first week, I could not get him out of my mind. I did not know that he was also thinking about me day and night. I never believed in telepathy until experiencing this special connection between us.

Our intimacy merged in sacredness through the spontaneous intelligence of our bodies and not through the thinking mind. I can feel the energy of his masculine part vibrating at a very high frequency within my feminine part. It was only years later when I experienced different states of vibrations through intense meditation practices that I came to understand that his body cells were already vibrating at the purest level of source energy.

My twin-flame and I have similarity in purpose and passion for life. We even somehow look similar to one another. We love each other more than anyone else, yet we are also each other's main trigger. Many times he triggers trauma deep inside me. This comes to the surface for eradication under the light of my pure consciousness. Indeed, in twin-flame relationships, dense and unconscious energies/traumas come to the surface to be eradicated. This is how one ascends to a higher level of cosmic consciousness with more space for freedom and wisdom to help fellow human beings in this ever evolving and expanding universe.

Many subsequent expansions of consciousness may seem negative in the beginning but will ultimately lead to greater wisdom, joy, and appreciation. The key is to make sure the light of consciousness is always on, as it is the source of all transformation and higher enlightenment. I find the more I appreciate an experience, the faster I transcend it. It is the secret to transform energy through the lights of love and pure consciousness. Twin-flame relationships, in my case, are supportive of higher levels of enlightenment or realization. Whether we are aware of it or not, we are all returning to love, the pure unconditional love that is worth experiencing. Love is the highest human experience, the state of Brahman. It is the highest frequency that Nirvana or Source can experience.

CHARACTERISTICS OF SOURCE

The characteristics of Source are unconditional love, purity, positivity, euphoria, expansion, and infinity. These states of oneness of energy are beyond the thinking mind. They are at the level of being and being free.

In the early journey of awakening, the mind often interprets one's experience. For example, right after experiencing cosmic love vibration, the mind may come in and try to understand what just happened, giving it names or label the experience itself. It normally takes maturity in one's journey to realize the difference between thought and direct experience, but for those who are ready, all it takes is a reminder from a realized one.

Action is nothing other than a direct projection of consciousness that one possesses at that moment. True Mastery is remaining rooted in states of Oneness while living in the world. When we squeeze a lemon, only lemon juice comes out. Squeezing an apple, apple juice comes out. Like that, when one is rooted in the oneness of unconditional love, there is no reason for hatred or separation to come out.

However, there are no fixed formulas to Mastery or those who are flowing through life as Source. Every moment, they are at their best. Challenges come as opportunities for them to ascend to higher wisdom, joy, appreciation, and mastery. A true Master is the one who can point to the mastery within each individual. That is the ultimate unconditional love.

ABOUT DEATH

Everyone is concerned about death at some point in their life. When I was a child I asked, "Grandma, does everyone including me have to die one day? And where do we go after we die?"

Up to this point, most of us have no certain or clear answer to this question. There are many people since antiquity, both spiritual and scientific, who were not religious, yet realized the Truth. What fascinates me is their truth synchronizing with the truth I find during my inner journey, and also synchronizing with the journey of those near and dear to me.

We often look for answers from family members, teachers, doctors, philosophers, neighbors, friends, etc. Enlightened Masters can also tell us about death.

Enlightened ones often don't believe what they are told. Mere belief in enlightenment is not enough. Experiencing enlightenment is what sets us free. Masters are those who take action to find the truth within themselves. Experiential truth is always available for those who seek it and take action.

"Every man possesses the Buddha Nature (Or everyone can realize Nirvana/ Enlightenment)" - Buddha

What I am about to share with you now is not only my direct experience about conscious death, but also the direct experience of my near and dear ones. Neuroscientists have shared information from hundreds of near death experiences in the recent years. Many cases were direct experience of scientists and neuroscientists themselves.

I attract what I am. In the recent years since I began on the conscious path of alignment. I have attracted living proof and evidence of higher consciousness. In this way, I attract evidence of consciousness after death.

DIRECT POINTER

Before we try to understand death, let's first understand life. What is life?

Please contemplate these questions/statements for a moment.

Is life itself an experience and only happening in the now?

Can life be divided into two experiences, the now and the experience?

The experience of consciousness can be sensed through: eyes, ears, noses, tongues, body, and mind.

Every moment is different, isn't it? The thought you had a few hours ago is now gone, isn't it? The more we are conscious, the more we see how fleeting this phenomena is.

The conscious experience is ever changing.

Consciousness and experiences are always coexisting.

When you are asleep, where does the consciousness go?

Only when the mental states arise, consciousness arises with it. It is called a dream state. However, during deep sleep, where does consciousness go?

Deep sleep is our true nature. It does not have a form of consciousness itself, however, it knows everything including consciousness. It is our true nature. Once Nirvana is consciously realized through the path of purification, or through adept Zen living, one will know this state of absolute and will know the state of deep sleep. It is the subtlest yet it is infinite. Only nothing can give birth to something. The infinite can give birth to the finite. For those who are adept, this realization is enough of truth itself.

SENSE DOORS

Alignment is a state of pure knowing, pure joy, and pure bliss. Perception at the purest level is also knowingness.

The purest levels of feelings is vibration and can also dissolve to consciousness/knowingness.

Thinking at the purest level is also vibration and can dissolve to conscious knowingness.

Everything is rooted in consciousness. That is my direct experience through meditation. In other words, through the practice of meditation, all denser frequencies of the body and mind are calmed down and unified within consciousness. Source or Nirvana is the state where consciousness itself also ceases.

After realizing my frequency automatically attracts those who vibrate at the same frequency, I discovered many beings such as Sri Nisargadatta Maharaj, Ramana Maharshi, Mojii, Papaji who can talk about this absolute dimension through direct experience. It is very interesting to know that when we are in certain alignment, we can recognize those who describe the unknown by their direct experience. Those who know can recognize others who know and those who don't. Those who see the truth can recognize each other for the Source is all knowing and is a very special quality of pure intelligence.

My path is not meant to be the only path. I believe there are people with different levels of consciousness existing in our current time. Let me share with you my little sister's story. She has been experiencing super-consciousness since she was a child (she is currently 25 years old). When she was young sleeping on a bus trip with our mother, she could recall everything that happened around her while her body was in deep sleep. Until this day, our family members learned not to do anything that they don't want my sister to know while she in in deep sleep because in the morning, she can report everything that happened. Her consciousness is never asleep, it is always awake.

My sister is not the only one with awakened consciousness during sleep. My very first Master also has this ability but developed this talent through meditation. My first Master practices mindfulness on breath. Every time I am around her, I feel peace, freshness because she is constantly absorbing peace and tranquility. The vibration of her presence is truly phenomenal. Abraham Hicks, the author of *Getting into the Vortex* said, "the process of breathing is much more than an essential function of your physical body. It is the flowing of Spirit to you, and through you".[6]

From 2016 - 2018 while I was practicing meditation in the forests of Myanmar, I noticed many scientists and psychotherapists, doctors, nurses, ect. from Western countries coming to practice. These were often the people who have access to advanced science. It is my joy to discover that during the past few years scientists also realize and are searching for deeper truths about consciousness especially the subject that concerns everyone: death.

DEATH AND SCIENCE

Dr. Sam Parnia is the Director of Resuscitation Research at NYU Langone School of Medicine in New York City. On the Doctor Oz show and on CBS News, Dr. Sam Parnia shared, "when the heart stops, all life processes go out because there is no more blood getting into the brain, into your kidneys, into your liver and we become lifeless, motionless. That is the time the doctors use to say time of death. What is really remarkable and has been discovered in the last 10 or 20 years is that after we die, after we go beyond the threshold of death that the cells inside the body start to decompose, they don't begin to decompose in the brain in the first few minutes. It can take many hours of time."

Knowing the scientific facts that cells start decomposing after the heart stops, his team discovered that they actually have a lot of time to bring people back, such as cooling the brain down, slowing down the rate by which cells die, restarting the heart again and reversing the process that causes them to die.

Except for people who commit suicide, those who die naturally, even if they were in pain before they died, the process of death becomes very comfortable, even blissful/peaceful. People describe a bright, warm, welcoming light that draws them towards it. They say sometimes relatives come to welcome them. In many cases they did not want to come back. It was so comfortable, like a magnet drawing them. A lot of them describe a sensation of separating from themselves and watching doctors and nurses working on them. They can hear things recall conversations, see everything and describe in clear detail what had happened.

Some describe that they reviewed everything that they had done to others by feeling that which others felt by their actions. At that time they get to judge themselves and realize what they should have done differently. Those who come back, tell the experience of what death was like for them. The profound thing is that they become transformed in a positive way. They see life very differently. They realize that life has more meaning, they have been given a second chance to do things differently. And by and large, they say that we should have tried to be of more service to others. Try to spend more time with families, try to help others much more, essentially be less self-centered, more altruistic. [1]

There are many other doctors, scientists, neuroscientists such as Dr. Eben Alexander, Dr. Mary Neal, Dr. Jill Botle Taylor, etc. just to name a few. New York Times best selling authors, who also shared their near death experience that synchronize with Dr. Sam Parnia's scientific discoveries.

A friend of mine in Houston experienced an out of body during meditation, and described it as unified divine pure unconditional love. She did not want to come back to human form.

In my direct experience through meditation, after the mental states along with solid perception of the body ceased, the only thing remaining was the purest infinite vibration of love and bliss - Brahman. After Brahman state ceased, the only thing left was the timeless absolute. These are the truest nature of who we are. When the perception of body and mental states ceased, it was pure bliss; I didn't want to exchange that state for human experience. I know those who left the body and only consciousness remained. The state is desirable. There should not be any fear about death because it is my experience and also hundreds of cases are proven about consciousness after death. Do we trust that or do we choose to trust in what we are told from some scriptures which are not necessarily from enlightened beings?

The point I am trying to make is, Nirvana is our source. We can never escape from Nirvana even if we want to. Later in this book, I will point to this deathless dimension that we are. Spirit or consciousness is pure bliss and love, a state of oneness. In my experience, it is the Brahman state of pure unconditional love and bliss. What do we have to lose when we leave the body? While being here, just live as if you have never lived, love as if you never loved, be happy as if happiness is the only choice you have.

Have a beautiful journey!

As we are already Source and never can we be separated from Source, any separation is because we believe so. Separation is a dimension of mind which is the duality of good/bad, right/wrong, ugly/pretty, and not the oneness which we are at our core. Duality is just there for us to experience and not be attached to.

From the position of our connectedness and well-being, we naturally start living a life of joy, and attract those of the same vibration. In my terms, that is the law of vibration, the law of attraction, the law of connectedness. That is when harmony, purpose, and fulfillment happen. A conscious life of a creator leads to a conscious death for we then consciously return to who we really are, the non-physical of unconditional love and freedom.

Source is the state of purity, it is the highest state that all beings can experience. It is the origin of who we really are and that can be found through meditation, the journey of turning inward. Anything that raises our frequency to higher love, bliss, balance and unity, is the way. Enjoy your journey.

THE CHART OF CONSCIOUSNESS BY

DR. DAVID HAWKINS

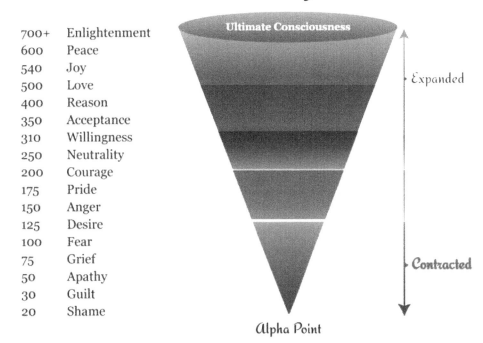

Omega

Ultimate Consciousness

700+	Enlightenment	
600	Peace	
540	Joy	Expanded
500	Love	
400	Reason	
350	Acceptance	
310	Willingness	
250	Neutrality	
200	Courage	
175	Pride	
150	Anger	
125	Desire	
100	Fear	Contracted
75	Grief	
50	Apathy	
30	Guilt	
20	Shame	

Alpha Point

Each level of consciousness coincides with determinable human behaviors and perceptions about life and the spiritual dimensions.

The following chart shows the low calibration of shame to the high calibration of enlightenment. The lower the calibration, the more contracted; the higher the calibration, the more expanded experience up until ultimate consciousness.

According to Dr. David Hawkins, currently, approximately 78% of the world's population is below the level of Courage (200).

Chart [3]

"The numbers on the scale represent logarithmic calibrations (measurable vibratory frequencies on a scale which increases to the tenth power) of the levels of human consciousness and its corresponding level of reality. The numbers themselves are arbitrary; the significance lies in the relationship of one number (or level) to another."

Some of the major crimes against humanity, such as the Holocaust, and the recent genocides in Bosnia and Rwanda could be said to have derived from Fear (100).

The 400s represent the level of reason, guided by the linear, mechanistic world of form (our modern society that includes advancements in medicine, science, government, etc.). Interestingly, the top echelon of intellectual genus, including Einstein, Freud, Newton, Aristotle, etc., all calibrated around 499.

From the level of Love (500), Hawkins claims only 0.4% of the population (1 in every 250 people) ever reach this level.

The Level of Peace (600) and above, this level is only attained by 1 out of 10 million people.

Not uncommonly, individuals at this level remove themselves from the world, as the state of bliss that ensues precludes ordinary activity. Some become spiritual teachers, others work anonymously for the betterment of mankind. A few become great geniuses in their respective fields and make major contributions to society.

Because the scale of consciousness is logarithmic, each incremental point represents a giant leap in power. One person calibrated at 700 (Enlightenment) counterbalances the negativity of 70 million people below 200. [4]

Along my journey of conscious alignment with source, my actions become spontaneous and love-based. The results of my actions are increasing happiness and wisdom. It truly is a path of joy and wellbeing. Synchronicities and miracles happen increasingly as I take action toward the well being of myself and others. All my needs are met while doing what I love. At times challenges come but the results always turn out positive because I face them through the eyes of oneness. That pure energy neutralizes all density and transforms it to wisdom.

In this conscious path, I realize that every moment I can choose to radiate the qualities that I want to multiply through thought, speech, and actions toward others.

Higher truths just keeps unfolding in my reality through people and circumstances. I am protected and loved by the universal energies of many blessed beings in our time who also walk the same path and understand the overwhelming happiness that I experience on the daily basis.

I want you all to know that you are loved and adored. Just be aware and find evidence of your infinite blessings.

MAHARISHI EFFECT

In the 1970s, using a rigorous scientific method, the Maharishi University sent groups of meditators to cities around the world where there were spots of conflict or crime. They found that when 1% of a community practiced the Transcendental Meditation, the crime rate was reduced by 16% on average.[9] The phenomenon was named the Maharishi Effect and was accepted for publication. It is proof that trained meditators doing group meditation can balance the surrounding energy for the better.

Now it makes total sense of why earlier years in my journey, I wanted to stay in meditation centers located in forests and mountains. It was the peaceful energy of love and harmony that I was addicted to. At such times, I noticed the difference between the energy of legitimate meditation centers compared with my home or marketplaces. Countries also have very unique energy fields. It is very noticeable to me every time I arrive in different airports. Imagine the world where everyone meditates. We would be living in a whole different world of heavenly frequency, love, peace, joy, and wisdom. Remember, meditation is not something that we have to DO. It is recognizing who we really are and thus navigate through a life of freedom and pure intelligence.

DR. MASARU EMOTO AND WATER CONSCIOUSNESS

Dr. Masaru Emoto is well-known for "water consciousness" where he discovered that water changes when purposely exposed to intentions such as love, compassion, gratitude, peace, etc. Under a microscope the water elements were beautifully symmetrical.

On the other hand, when water is exposed to negative intentions, tap water, heavy metal music, etc., the elements distorted in ugly asymmetrical structures.

Everything affects everything at the energy level. We are all connected whether we are aware of it or not. The Maharishi experiment along with this water consciousness experiment are proof that our thoughts and emotions do affect us, others, and the surrounding environment either positively or negatively. Our bodies are after all 75% water.

When we speak positive empowering words, it does affect the feelings and emotions of others. Everything is connected on many levels, all it takes is awareness to realize this. The truth is always around us. Mindfulness is a beautiful and joyful way to experience life. When we are conscious, old energies are purified or transformed, new wholesome habits of joy and higher alignment begin. We naturally start filling our lifes with more kind words, thought, and actions. This called the conscious path or awakened path. Only then, a new world, a beautiful world appears because a beautiful world is formed by the combination of beautiful people.

CONSCIOUSNESS EVOLUTION

These days we begin learning about science early in school, taking classes in physics and chemistry. Under a microscope, atoms were discovered as the building blocks of all matter. Science has discovered four or more states of matters: solid, liquid, gas, and plasma. For example a solid ice cube after melting becomes liquid/water, liquid/water after boiling becomes vapor or gas. When applying very strong heat to gas it becomes plasma. An example of plasma is when an electric current passes through fluorescent light bulbs or neon signs. When an electrical current is passed through the mercury vapor in fluorescent light bulbs, it heats up the gas sufficiently to strip the electrons and to create plasma (light).

Human evolution has done a great job in converting nature's resources such as sunlight and water to electricity or energy that allows us to have the comfort of lights, refrigerators, cellphones, cars, etc. However, we are always in the process of expansion. Fifty years ago, if I told my friend that I could use a small, thin device to talk with other humans in a different country in Asia, no one would have believed me because cell phones were not available. If I had a smartphone back then I might be seen as one with psychic abilities. Same as with airplanes one hundred years ago. If you told your friend that you could use a flying device and travel from the USA to India in one day, your friend would most likely tell you "good luck with your wild imagination". Many things that we experience today would be seen as psychic back then when humans had not yet discovered these things. Imagine the possibilities we will have fifty years from now.

Scientists are continuously in the process of discovery. I notice that many of the meditators that I have met all over the world are themselves doctors, scientists, psychotherapists, lawyers, etc. They explore meditation because of the continuous scientific discoveries about mind, matter, and consciousness.

I realize that many of our scientific discoveries were inspired by the inner discoveries of enlightened masters such as Buddha. The only difference is that the enlightened beings discovered the deepest truth and possibilities by going inside, not through any devices or outer experiments. About 2600 years ago, Buddha had already discovered subatomic particles (Rupa Kalapa was the Pali term that he used in his time). He also experienced different realms of reality that science later discovered and refer to as different levels of frequencies. Buddha also talked about the law of cause and effect which is the law of attraction. We attract what we put out to the universe. He also taught about Source or Nirvana which we now call the zero point or consciousness, or the absolute, etc. Recently I watched a talk conducted at Mind-Valley University in Tallinn by Nassim Haramein with more than 30 years research in physics. He has written multiple papers and appeared on the TEDx Talks show. He said, "each proton is connected to all other protons in the universe, all the information in the universe is present in each one of them. If you want to actually know about the universe, go inside yourself".

This is the reason why masters discovered the wisdom or solution to all life challenges by going inside. I find this is also true in my direct experience. Though minds are different among individuals, how the mind works is the same, and the mechanism to master it is also the same. Our true nature is within, rooted in a no-self state. It is possible, with effort, for anyone to clearly see the mind, its behaviors/functions and use it effectively. It is the key difference between masters and others. Others are being used by the mind, a psychological term called ego. Source however is selfless, it is pure nature, pure consciousness, it is no-self. Only when we are free from our mind can we use it effectively. Otherwise, it controls our emotions, behaviors, our life itself.

It is very interesting to know that the more I see how my mind works, the more clearly I see how other people's minds work because the mechanism is the same. Some call this a psychic ability, being able to read the mind of others. I believe this is simply a natural ability we all realize when we go inside ourselves. Back before humans had written language, they knew exactly the best time to plant seeds. The calendar was made by humans and it is fascinating to see how they knew that the 15th of every lunar month, the moon is perfectly round. Because we were originally connected with the whole, we knew how nature works. We could sense it or in other words, connect with it. Everything is me quantumly, like now, I can be anywhere in the universe that I want because it is the same substance. It is all me, my consciousness. We cannot know something that is outside our consciousness. Our consciousness is all there is, the oneness energy or knowing.

When dogs in my hometown in Vietnam are sick, they can go around the village and eat natural plants that heal them. Many Chinese medicines were discovered in the same way by the wisdom of ancient people. They taste the plant and know which part of the body it will heal. Animals still retain this sense of connectedness. As many dog lovers will know, dogs don't judge you, they love you unconditionally. Being itself is a sense of unconditional love. Being around the beingness of a dog can help us feel more connected and grounded with who we really are at the level of being. That is why so many love their dogs. Through evolution, humans were gifted the ability of spoken language which has an strong impact on ourselves and others. Therefore it is very important to speak empowering/ kind words, of love and infinite possibilities to remind us our true powers. Enlightened people consciously choose to live their life joyfully. They are conscious in thoughts, speech, and action because thoughts, speech, and actions are unique in the human world. If each human would consciously choose thoughts, words, and actions that are loving and empowering toward well being of oneself and others, imagine the world that we would live in. No more wars, fights, jealousy, hatred, etc. Science has proven that we are all connected at the energy level. The previous water consciousness experiment and Maharishi effects prove this.

ENERGY

Everything is energy. Those who have done meditation, especially Vipassana, can feel different forms of energy through body sensations or movement of the breath. The purer the mind is, the subtler are ones vibrations. At the subtlest level of the material world, it is pure energy. Everything is vibrations, and vibration itself is the movement of particles. Advanced meditators see this, not merely believe it. What I share in this book speaks from direct experience and can be proven by scientists if they are willing to explore it. There are also my near and dear ones who experience the same or higher states of reality. My Master is already free from the cycle of birth and death. He also reached different levels of consciousness and mastery including seeing Akashic records, auras and mind waves.

Breath itself has form, it is pure white and can be seen with or without open eyes. I witnessed that in my ten-day meditation course in Myanmar. The ancient ones called it Prana, the life force. Breath is not such a simple thing. The energy of breath is very strong. I can see and feel it when in a deep state of concentration. I've seen that breath is made up of space particles white in color.

Our body constantly consumes and transforms food to energy. The breath constantly flows in and out whether we are aware of it or not. This pure energy also sustains our life. The more conscious we are, the subtler we experience this reality.

At some point we will experience divinity at the core of all life forms.

Consciousness is the awareness of life energy or life experiences. Depending on the level of consciousness, one experiences reality at a grosser or subtler level. Consciousness is universal and it is one. When we operate from consciousness level, we naturally realize the oneness, the universal intelligence of love, harmony, compassion, joy, and wisdom. All it takes is alignment with who we really are.

THE POWER OF WORDS

It takes energy to talk, think, and act. The wise are those who consciously/mindfully use their energy most effectively (or wisely). Energy transforms. Words we speak are a form of energy that can affect/transform ourselves and the surroundings. One of the paths from the Noble Eight Fold Path taught by Buddha is right speech. It is very important because the way we use words shapes our reality. It is simple cause and effect. Thoughts, actions, and speech are expressions of our belief system and our subconscious mind. To form a new belief system or subconscious mind and create reality that we want, it takes conscious awareness. Consciously using high vibration thoughts, speech, and actions automatically takes care of your new reality. We attract what we are and what we radiate through thoughts, speech and actions. High vibration attracts like energy and helps form a new reality of that higher frequency. It is the path of the conscious creator.

In 2018 during an intensive retreat in Yangon Myanmar, I noticed for a period of time, sounds that people spoke became vibrations. They vibrated and penetrated through my ears and body because at that time my body itself was also vibrating. Everything is always vibrating and working that way but only when my concentration or awareness is sharply align, the truth is perceived at that subtle level. At that time I was a bit concerned because I could not understand conversations normally because they were all vibrations to me. But actually I was cared for by the universe in the most beautiful way. I was happy, joyful, and radiant. Life was so vibrant/alive and connected at that time. One afternoon I was on the 4th floor looking down on the open kitchen below. There were volunteers selflessly cooking and washing dishes so hundreds of meditators could have a peaceful retreat. At that time I was feeling the vibration of one of the volunteers. It was so clear that my vibration vibrated inside her body. I was one with her. I cried blissful tears of unconditional love and connectedness.

POINTERS TO THE MOON

Truth is like the masters pointing to "the moon" during their teachings. Once one sees "the moon" or realizes/sees the truth, the finger is no longer necessary. Enlightenment is indeed universal and can be realized by anyone regardless of educational background, religion, country, rich or poor, good or bad.

Everyone has a true origin that is called true nature or Source, the deathless dimension within, or the Nirvanic peace beyond duality. In a broader perspective, everything falls within the ultimate truth itself, including all religions, countries, lives and all things. Everything in this universe is a small part of the infinite. Once Truth is consciously recognized, wisdom is naturally activated and then one lives the life of freedom beyond all duality bondages and limitations. Life returns to the spontaneous flow of pure joy and intelligence. The source gives birth to all there is. It is the infinite creation that is unfolding new possibilities every-moment in this dynamic, alive universe. Humans are the tools for this dynamic unfolding of universal infinite intelligence.

Pure intelligence of the universe is beyond measure, it gives life and is life itself. For example, whether we are aware of the breath or not, the breath happens on its own to keep us alive. Which force do you think makes this happen? Small cuts on the skin automatically heal themselves after a few days. What force is behind such healing? The sun and earth don't crash into one another. What force is behind this? The Sun gives light, warmth, and energy to life on earth without asking for anything in return. Science itself has proven that we are energy. Each being is part of the whole, the pieces of the puzzle that make up the total picture of this infinite intelligent life force. We are part of this infinite game. This infinite game is governed by frequency at the deepest level, the law of energy or the law of attraction (cause and effect). Knowing this secret, one starts consciously creating the game of reality that one wishes to experience before returning to the origin of who we really are, the Nirvana before existence. Realizing the Nirvanic dimension or source and flow in life as that is a blessing.

EGO

Ego is the result of accumulated thoughts and the beliefs about it. Thoughts themselves are fleeting and impermanent. Believing that we are the mental states/thoughts is the result of not knowing who we really are. Once we realize that we are not our thoughts and emotions, we start recognizing through awareness the deeper truth of who we really are. Knowing that we are not thoughts and emotions, we are free from their control. The Source that we are is the pure knowingness that is universal intelligence itself. Being at one with Source, we start understanding the secret of the universe, and how it works. This process of discovery gives us clarity and wisdom to take charge of our life experience as a conscious Creator. Everything is energy and everything is connected. Alignment with Source gives us access to all the secrets of the universe. The hidden secrets unfolding in one's experience is fascinating, joyful, and fulfilling. The internal guidance within is the true and the last Master of yours, no one else. The Masters of all time did the same thing, they aligned with Source intelligence, the internal guidance within.

THAT WHICH WE ALL REALLY WANT

Everyone wants happiness, right?

Everyone who follows enlightened masters or the religions that were established to worship their saintly qualities does so because deep down we respect and wish to be happy and blissful like them. We believe that when we practice their teachings we can live a happy life or when we die, we can go to heaven or Nirvana. So the origin of what we really want is happiness, correct? If Nirvana or heaven would cause pain and suffering, who would worship and follow such a path? I am sure the reason all beings including enlightened masters follow the path of enlightenment, is to find long lasting happiness of heaven or Nirvana.

Not limited to spirituality, one may claim to be a fan of a certain singer because their music makes us feel good. We enjoy their work because it makes us feel happy. If their song irritated or upset you, are you still a fan?

Same with relationships. Love is irresistible to everyone because love and intimacy feels good. We love the feeling of joy, bliss, and happiness. If sex and intimacy felt bad, would we want it?

How about finances? Why do we love or want money? Have you ever asked yourself that question? Contemplation is the source of all wisdom. Ask and it is given because the law of attraction starts attracting those who can answer the question. Isn't the reason why we love money because it can be used to buy a beautiful house, comfortable car, a wonderful vacation, and the things that bring higher comfort, joy, and happiness to our experience? So the underlying reason for loving and wanting money is the desire for comfort, joy, and happiness.

So, what we all want are JOY and HAPPINESS, right?

SOURCE

So what is truth? Truth is the ultimate freedom dimension and is the root of all existence. Truth or Source itself is infinite and limitless and it does not belong to the duality/polarity dimension. Source is the subtlest of all forms. It is formless and timeless.

Buddhism teaches Anatta (Selflessness/Non-self). It defines perfectly the dimension of Source which is beyond individuality or false sense of ego.

God represents infinite love, intelligence, and power. Source itself is God, for it is the Source of all there is, including you. You are, we are, always connected with God/Source, the pure unconditional love and infinite intelligence that gives birth and life to all there is. Learning the law of source (the law of attraction), one lives in alignment with the intelligence of God/Source that you originally are.

Soul represents Oneness and infinite love. Soul is Source. It is nonphysical oneness. Soul is always connected to Nirvana. Mahayana Buddhism teaches about the three bodies of Buddha. Using modern terms, I call them: 1. human (duality/ego). 2. Soul, the Celestial, Brahman or oneness of unconditional love and bliss. One returns to this dimension after leaving the body. 3. Nirvana, the ultimate no time-space dimension, the origin of the first two dimensions.

Source itself is beyond words, for words themselves are not a direct experience of Source. Belief in the words or teaching is not enough. Only directly experiencing Source removes all doubts, delusions, and sufferings.

DIFFERENT LEVELS OF ENERGY AND CONSCIOUSNESS

"If you want to find the secrets of the Universe, think in terms of energy, frequency, and vibration." - Nikola Tesla

For those adept in science or meditation, you know that everything is energy and energy does not die, it just transforms. Source is not energy/subatomic particles. It is the Absolute before all manifestation of energy. Energy is the projection of the Absolute. Absolute itself is nothing. Because the Absolute is nothing, it is the origin of all things. All things are a projection of the universe experiencing its intelligent power of infinite possibilities. That which is nothing and infinite, can give birth to anything. That which is something, itself is a limitation of that something. This infinite possibility is governed by the law of attraction (cause and effect). That which is like unto itself, is drawn. We, at every moment, attract and experience what we are vibrating. It is important to take charge of our vibration by becoming conscious of who we really are (Source/Creator). Only then can we understand energy (body/mind mechanism) and be able to use it for the highest good.

At the level of Source (the origin of all things) we perceive the world at a more intuitive level, at an energy or vibration level. Everything is connected and governed by the law of attraction and this becomes more and more clear as one goes deeper. Masters are those who have a choice of how they want to perceive life. It is not what happens that dictates their experience because they are not rooted in duality but in Source, the infinite freedom and creative dimension beyond experience itself. The true experiencer or perceiver is always free.

When we are at source level and not attached to any particular phenomena, we perceive with absolute clarity and this is how Buddha and enlightened beings perceive life.

THE RULE OF CONSCIOUSNESS

The rule of consciousness is that the finer dimension can perceive grosser ones, but the grosser dimension cannot perceive the higher ones. The enlightened ones can see exactly at which states of reality you operate but you can't see their state unless you are in alignment with their state or higher. All masters who are rooted in Source, can recognize one another. That is why the more in alignment we are, the wiser and clearer we are. The highest state is Source or Oneness. Oneness can perceive all dimensions with clarity. Enlightened Beings are rooted in the Source, and that is why we call them "the wise". We all can access this dimension of clarity for it is you at the core. The difference between enlightened beings and others is the recognition of this truth. Enlightened masters realized that they are the source while others think that the stories in their mind about themselves is reality.

ONENESS AND ABILITIES

Being in alignment with Source, one starts directly experiencing the true meaning of divinity. Besides bliss, joy, happiness, and mastery, psychic ability, accessed from ones connectedness with all there is, is just a "side benefits" of alignment with Source. The clearest example I can site is provided by Esther Hicks, the queen of Law of Attraction teaching. As she allows Abraham, the non-physical dimension of pure love and intelligence to speak through her, she accesses psychic abilities such as channeling, clairvoyance, and telepathy with the audiences. Abraham's guidance is always spot-on, for it comes from the nonphysical Source that connects with us all. That is why the teaching brings so much joy, freedom, and connectedness with the whole.

I recognize these abilities in other spiritual beings because I also witness the same truth in myself when I am in alignment with Source. The discovery has become more satisfying every day, especially in the past two years as I started receiving wisdom or information that is from other parts of the world. The only thing I can really do now is to allow the universe to unfold this mysterious life. It is so far beyond my thinking mind that I decided five years ago to let go of it. I choose to experience life with intuition (universal intelligence or wisdom) rather than the limited mental memories, the circle of karma.

What fascinates me the most is that the more challenges I experience, the greater is my love, understanding, and appreciation of life. Life is no longer suffering. Everything from this point is naturally converted to love and wisdom.

The state of oneness allows me to connect and feel others' mind and emotion. As I open up more to life, I see people suffering what I suffered years ago. The connectedness or oneness love I have for others is the fuel for my creativity, passion, and power to stand up and speak the truth that has set me free.

I had never expected that my true purpose would reveal itself through challenges and feeling the pain of others. Life gets tastier everyday as truth reveals itself with greater intensity. The truth that I speak of is the fabric of love and bliss. I know this, through conviction, is what we are truly made of.

WHO ARE WE?

We are eternal. We are Source experiencing itself in human form. We are infinite potential once we recognize and allow this dimension of our true origin to unfold. The human body and mind are our tools to experience creation. We are the royal princes and princesses of the Universe. Our origin is perfect purity, freedom, and unconditional love. We are the experiencers of life.

WHO ARE WE NOT?

The mental states of judgment, comparison, hatred, and separation never end because anything we believe adds energy to magnify it. The Universal law of attraction will respond by attracting and manifesting the same energy that we radiate. The ego or fleeting mental states is duality, not oneness, not us.

Reprogramming the subconscious mind is the key to recognizing our true source of perfect purity. The accumulated thoughts or belief systems will resolve themselves under the light of pure consciousness, because energy doesn't die, it transforms. This is the path of all the wise that humans worship. Masters grounded in Source spontaneously radiate peace, joy, and calmness. All transformation happens naturally by that purest frequency of love, bliss, and freedom.

PERCEPTION DICTATES EXPERIENCE

Often we view the world through our own level of perception. For example, reality perceived through the "eyes" of Jesus or Buddha is full of love, oneness, and wisdom for they are grounded in Source or Nirvana. Those who are free from the mind will be able to choose how they want to experience life. That is true mastery.

Otherwise, we perceive others and circumstances through the lenses of a limited belief system and not Source intelligence. Belief system is a set of accumulated life experiences that happened in the past. By not knowing and being grounded in who we are, we identify ourselves to be the circumstance itself. Life circumstances change and have no root. Experiences of loss, confusion, and stress are the result of seeing oneself as something that is impermanent and rootless.

The wise are those who recognize the true root or Source within, the state of true freedom beyond all life challenges and circumstances. Source is always fresh, balanced, and is open to infinite possibilities. Source cannot be beaten, for it has no form. As a person, one can be harmed physically or mentally but as Source, one cannot be harmed.

INFINITE POSSIBILITY, OUR TRUE STRENGTH

Because Source is always new and infinite at every moment, those who are in alignment with Source automatically access infinite potential. It is not how many times we fail, it is how many times we stand back up. When in alignment with Source, one stands back up every time with higher wisdom, freedom, and love to all. The taste of this is blissfully beautiful.

The nature of Source is fearless. As an experiencers, we are not here to fix anything broken, we are here to live as the creator that we truly are. We can create anything that we can imagine. Imagination is our true wings. By living the life of a conscious and joyous creator, we naturally inspire those creators around us by just being who we are, living a life that we are meant to, a life worth living.

CONNECTEDNESS

As One recognizes and flows in life as Source, one experiences connectedness through synchronicities, increasing appreciation, love, intimacy, and beauty. My journey involves many blissful tears as the discovery gets better and deeper all the time. This is the path of infinite joy.

VIBRATIONS

Source is the highest vibration of all, the subtlest of the subtle. It is divinity and it is our true nature. The reason why we love pleasant feelings is because pleasant feelings such as love, bliss, joy, compassion, creativity, inspiration, etc. are closer to the subtlest or finest vibration that we really are. That is why we love it, we feel comfortable, or in other words, feel at "home". We like it because the higher frequency we experience, the closer to Source alignment we are, and it feels good.

The same goes for sex. True tantric sex can bring one to the state of cosmic consciousness, the state of perfect alignment. Whether we are aware of it or not, we love the experience of wholeness and wellbeing right after the peak of orgasm. Sex causes an increase of oxytocin which is the love hormone and endorphins which are natural pain killing hormones.

"If you want to find the secrets of the Universe, think in terms of energy, frequency, and vibration." - Nikola Tesla

Through a pure, sharp mind, the wise perceive reality as frequency, either low or high. There is no such thing as right or wrong in the dimension of vibration. Nirvana is the highest and purest dimension of all and is ultimate bliss. That is why we say enlightened ones search for Nirvana. We prefer bliss over pain and suffering. Bliss are states of heaven and celestial frequencies. On the other hand, sufferings or pain are states of low frequencies.

Let's discuss the process of orgasm and why sex is irresistible to everyone. When a couple get started, the experience of love and being loved triggers the expansion/euphoric feeling of love and being loved which is in itself high frequency. When moving to sexual intercourse, joy increases by focus, continuity, and intensity. At it's peak, orgasm happens and one experiences the state of wholeness (perfect ying-yang balance). Right after orgasm, the state of perfect alignment takes over the ego or compulsive thoughts. One experiences absolute stillness and fulfillment. We enjoy sex because of the sense of returning "home" and fulfillment which is our natural state when we let go of the ego/compulsive thoughts.

Enlightened people know the keys to alignment and can consciously enter blissful states without the necessity of sex. We humans enjoy sex because it leads to the state of infinite expansion/euphoria and unification with Source/God. An enlightened person experiences life to the fullest compared with others because they know how to sense life at the deepest level. They can choose sexual intimacy, but their action is conscious, and can lead their partner to the same state of conscious unification/ fulfillment. Energy is always interconnected and can be felt during intimacy with a soulmate. When their partner is in expansive bliss which overrides the ego, the state of expansive consciousness easily picks up the cosmic consciousness of their partner who is already in alignment with Source. This often happens in twin-flame or conscious couples. This indeed is the very high level of metaphysics where everything is interconnected. During orgasm, enlightened ones enjoy it to the fullest because they experience life at a cellular level. Every one of their cells becomes affected by the orgasm. The oneness state of orgasm at the cellular level is not limited to the body, it is infinite. Enlightened people truly get the most out of life. This simple key itself can make them feel euphoric at their core, the vibration or cellular level.

We frequently experience cosmic consciousness right after orgasm. We don't know why or we aren't consciously aware of this state. As one practices mindfulness, especially realizing it's true nature, this state of consciousness becomes clearer and clearer in one's awareness. Sex can lead us "home", align us with Source, because sex itself involves so many frequencies of love, joy, intimacy, and inclusiveness (oneness).

In opposition to high frequency states, are low frequency states such as hatred, jealousy, and anger. These are the realms of separation and are far away from the oneness that we truly are. They carry us further away to grosser experiences and greater sense of loss and imbalance. That is why no one likes to experience anger, hatred, jealousy, and animosity, for these states are not in alignment with who we really are.

CONNECTEDNESS AND GENIUSES

In many of Abraham Hicks' books, it states that, "we are pure positive energy. Happiness or a sense of wellbeing is not something that we have to achieve or reach for, it is already our true nature. The path of alignment is to let go of the outdated, limiting beliefs that cover the true happiness and pure intelligence that we are. The outdated files of compulsive thoughts (judgment, comparison, limiting perspectives, etc.) do nothing but slow down our progress like clouds covering our true natural state of freedom, intelligence, and joy.

Anything other than Source is just a temporary experience. The process of enlightenment is realigning ourselves with who we really are and consciously creating the reality of love, joy, happiness, and fulfillment that we are here to enjoy.

The direction in which the crowd is heading is not necessarily the right direction. Those who have higher vision of life and truth like Buddha and Jesus took action to find the right direction, to "know thyself". This is the source of infinite intelligence and unconditional love or inclusiveness. Those who are connected with their purpose and passion have access to exceptional amounts of creativity, beauty, and intelligence. I remember watching Jeff Bezos, the CEO of Amazon, in an interview and he mentioned the importance of having the beginner's mind. Whether he is aware of it or not, a beginner's mind is truly a Zen mind, God's mind, the mind of a Creator. I am not aware of any exceptionally successful person who is not aware of their power and trust in the "voice" within.

THE INNER VOICE

Exceptional people are those who "listen" to the voice within. Only you know what triggers you, what you are best at, what you love and what inspires you toward passion, joy, and fulfillment. You are the one who lives with you all the time, no one else can. The outside voices are opinions of others with their own personal life experiences and are not your truth. Even among enlightened people, I have never seen any two that have had the exact same journey to enlightenment. Another thing that all enlightened beings have in common is cultivating their connection with Source. There is no point in fighting about the differences. We must realize that truth is universal and is the path to all wisdom and fulfillment. No one has the same path, every human is creator of their own reality. True masters are the ones who can point others to their ultimate master within. Your ultimate master within is one and the same with your master's master.

YOUR TRUE PROTECTION

Our wisdom is our true protection. When we are in alignment with Source, we will recognize information that triggers love and bliss as well as information that triggers fear and guilt. We are creators of our reality and whatever we give attention to and believe in grows. When we give attention to something, it becomes our reality right at that moment and also attracts similar vibration to strengthen the life of that energy and eventually become a belief, and so the process multiplies. It is important to nourish our Soul/life with attention to love, joy, wisdom, and harmony, which will naturally blossom by the law of nature. We can't resist sharing such beauty of divinity with the Whole for we are already rooted in oneness love.

THE JOYFUL PATH

When one is in alignment with Source, the path becomes joyful and effortless. One flows through life with ease, joy, wisdom, connectedness, and gratitude. It does not mean that one does not have challenges, but challenges come as opportunities for one to advance to higher love, intelligence, and expansion.

THE BEST VACATION

The idea of vacation is meant to help one relax, refresh and reconnect with happiness, joy, and passion for life.

Stress is a lack of mastery, not knowing our true place. Those who are connected to the Source, produce better results because of clarity of mind and not being controlled or slowed down by stress. Source is a dimension of freshness beyond all mental states. Many meditators I have met along my journey shared how meditation has helped them become more productive, happy, harmonious, and balanced in their business and personal life. The best vacation is truly a vacation within. Once that dimension is activated, a vacation place can be anywhere. One enjoys existence and vacation at a deeper level, life itself becomes your vacation when you flow as source energy.

EMOTIONAL MASTERY

When we lack mastery, just about anyone in the world can dictate/affect our emotions. Many people look for approval outside, like a smile from others in order to feel happy and loved. The truth is not everybody can give us a smile all the time. Often they themselves are looking for a smile and acceptance from others for their happiness. Since ancient times many have taken action to find the true happiness and mastery within because their "inner guidance" knows it is possible.

Those who connect with passion, kindness, and motivation are always happy and energetic. I myself for many years was told that I am always happy, energetic, and raise positive energy in the room. I was also able to manifest what I wanted in life with ease. I did not know why back then but I do now after years of going inside myself. I radiated joy and happiness, I magnified it and that high frequency is a state of openness and allowing manifestation of abundance and wellbeing. Now after years of meditation, I find my happiness has increased many fold. This huge difference is because now I know how to master my mind and emotions which I did not know back then prior to meditation and the inner journey.

MASTERY

One of the values of religion is to help life be more balanced and joyful. This is more important than the heaven/Nirvana that is somewhere in the future. Every moment can be either heaven or a hell depending on the individual's perception. But for a master it is a conscious choice.

A master's life is not less challenging than other people's, because without challenges life cannot lead one to greater wisdom and realization. The top masters I have come into contact with experienced extreme challenges in their journey and that is exactly why they evolved. The only difference between them and others is that they face experience as Source. Everything that emanates from that is love, pure intelligence (wisdom) and understanding. All that comes from the masters is true spontaneous intelligence of Source. It is beyond the thinking mind. True mastery points you to the master within. They may not solve all your problems but they will point you to the master inside that has answers to all your questions for the rest of your life. Eventually you will realize that there is no such thing as a "problem". That is true compassion of a Master.

It is not about what happens, it is how they choose to perceive/experience what happens that is their mastery. As they live in the state of Source or flow of life, everything is viewed as oneness and freedom. Therefore, wisdom, understanding, and compassion deepen when they face life challenges. They allow the spontaneous intelligence of Source experiencing itself in human form. They are indeed selfless. That makes a true Master. They control their inner world, their ego.

There are many who see masters still facing challenges in life and judge them based on that. The truth is, after enlightenment, masters really taste the beauty of life. They can experience the extreme realities but both dualities are equally tasty to the masters. They are opportunities to evolve to more infinite wisdom and love. The more challenges they experience, the more love and depth they acquire in order to help others become free from similar situations. Wisdom always knows what to do and comes out stronger/better.

THE EXERCISE, AWARE THE QUESTIONER

In this exercise, as you are ask questions, it is recommended to be aware of the "questioner". The questioner or the person who acts, thinks, knows, loves, hates, ect., is not you. It is known by who you really are. You are Source, so stay balanced and aware of the questioner.

Let's get started:

Who am I?
Am I the body?
Am I the mind?
Am I the questioner?
Am I conscious?
Am I unconscious?

Am I thought?

Am I the thinker?

Am I happy?

Am I suffering?

Am I liberated?

Am I bound?

Am I jealous?

Am I proud?

Am I the victim?

Am I the winner?

Am I the loser?

Am I beautiful?

Am I ugly?

Am I love?

Am I the beloved?

Am I hatred?

Am I the contentment?

Am I restless?

Am I ?

Am I at peace?

Am I discontented?

Am I free?

Am I the delusion?

Am I mundane?

Am I super mundane ?

Am I the mother?

Am I the father?

Am I the sister?

Am I the brother?

Am I the In-laws?

Am I "good enough"?

Am I "not good enough"?

Am I in doubt?

Am I wise?

Am I a fool?

Am I rich?

Am I poor?

Am I the baby?

Am I an adult?

Am I a success?

Am I a failure?

Am I orgasmic?

Am I an illness?

Am I a wellbeing?

Am I behaving badly?

Am I behaving well?

Am I fortunate?

Am I unfortunate?

Am I the greatness?

Am I the listener?

Am I the speaker?

Am I angry?

Am I sweet?

Am I hungry?

Am I fulfilled?

Am I satisfied?

Am I the disciple?

Am I the master?

Am I God?

Am I an angel?

Am I Source?

Am I a human?

Am I ordinary?

Am I the power?

Am I useless?

Am I enjoying it?

Am I dissatisfied?

Am I an impermanence?

Am I the permanence?

Am I energy?

Am I successful?

Am I a failure?

Am I dispassionate?

Am I passionate?

Am I wise?

Am I a fool?

Am I a new born child?

Am I male/female?

Am I 11 years old?

Am I 22 years old?

Am I 66 years old?

Am I the one in this body now?

Am I my profession?

Am I my professional title?

Am I the fulfilled?

Am I unfulfilled?

Am I bored?

Am I excited?

Am I doing some wholesome action?

Am I doing some unwholesome action?

Am I doing a good deed?

Am I doing a bad deed?

Am I the fear?

Am I brave?

Am I a sinner?

Am I a Saint?

......

Did you notice the mind tried to contemplate and answer the questions?

Did you notice the negative words have power and can affect the emotion?

Did you notice that thinking takes a lot of energy?

Did you notice there was an overwhelming mental state of confusion by not knowing all the answers?

Did you notice the witness that was silence and perceive the questioner, the answer, the confusion, and the emotion?

Are you now noticing that you are aware of your thoughts and thinking?

Does that awareness have a size or shape or form?

Every time you look for awareness, do you notice that the looker is also perceived by the complete silence?

That complete silence before all forms of consciousness is Source. It is the absolute. It is neither time nor space. It is not known but through the known, it can be recognized.

Now every time you enter meditation, or while walking or during daily activities, just be aware of the silence. Aware of your thinking, thoughts, emotions, actions, and speech. Master that first.

During sitting meditation, you can be aware of the awareness itself. That is the gate to the absolute.

For those who have access to the OM sound, be aware of that sound during sitting meditation. That is the fastest path to the absolute in my direct experience. The second time I experienced the absolute in Myanmar that cosmic sound was the only prominent thing, and it led me to the absolute. The famous lotus sutra talks about this cosmic sound and how it can lead one to true nature.

When in alignment, one has the answers to all questions, because Source is infinite possibility and knows everything. Everything is energy. One can create what one wants to experience in life for one's belief shapes one's reality based on law of attraction of energy/vibration. As Source, one becomes a creator, a designer of one's reality. Source has no form therefore everything is possible. Conscious creation of reality is the path to enlightenment.

Surrendering to or allowing Source is a very high state of consciousness. It is when wisdom reaches maturity of understanding how reality works and connects at the energy level. Our true place is pure, positive energy. This is the secret to a fulfilled life. It does not mean that suffering does not exist. It is how we consciously choose to direct our attention to the suffering. We are multi-dimensional. Everything is a habit and once we start forming new habits as the conscious creators it becomes fun.

Surrender the limiting ego that is trying to figure out wisdom and connectedness with life energy. With some people, ego naturally surrenders because of painful life experiences. The state of allowing Source is engaging your true divinity. You have nothing to lose, you came here naked and perfectly happy, you will go back to the same place that you are. There is nothing to lose. It is either allowing your divinity to unfold or continue living a limited life of ego.

After realizing who we are originally, we have the right to claim a life of infinite possibilities. That which is nothing or infinite has potential to create something. That which is something already limits creation of something new.

THE SOURCE THAT I AM

All lives are the reflection of I AM, the manifestation of our true selves. All Beings hold the key to Source intelligence, the intelligence of all knowing.

All lives can never be separated from Source for it is the origin of all.

Source is undefinable. Source does not care what you call it or how you define it because it is formless and infinite. The formless/infinite can be filled with love or hate. However, when one knows how to flow in life as Source, everything that is experienced in this dimension automatically transforms to purity, love, and wisdom. Conscious creators never choose hate over love for conscious creators are those who are naturally in alignment with the highest frequencies which can never attract low frequencies unless they choose to.

Source has no form, no place, no sensation, no perception, no thought, no awareness and is the origin of all.

Source is Zen, Buddha, Jesus, enlightenment, freedom, liberation, oneness, ultimate bliss, Nirvana, God, etc. These are different names that humans choose to define Source or the ones that have realized Source. All is Source.

Source is one's true nature, already free, already liberated. Nirvana is beyond all concepts.

DIRECT POINTER

Dear sisters and brothers, if you have read the previous pages, you may be aware of the infinite dimension of no time/no space that is you. It is a state of deep sleep that is the Nirvana we experience every night and everyday. We are always connected with Source. The difference between enlightened Beings and others is that enlightened beings are conscious of the existence of this dimension and allow it to be who they are, and not the ego. This dimension is indeed the state of no-self because it has no form and is beyond normal senses or even consciousness itself.

What we have been searching for is always with us. The mind often looks for something extraordinary, outside the self. The truth is, this infinite dimension gives birth to all possibilities. That makes it extraordinary. For example, when our hand is full, we cannot hold anything else but with an empty hand it is possible to hold other things of our choice. Just like that, when the mind is so full of duality concepts, there is no space for higher dimensions of true love and unity.

"By letting go, it all gets done" - Lao Tzu.

Letting go means relieving yourself of ego. Only when we let go of the ego can Source then have a vessel to flow into. Those who recognize the Source of who they are, have a choice to free themselves from the heaviness of mental states. Source is a dimension of clarity and perfect alignment with the universal law of vibration.

A BEAUTIFUL LIFE

Spirituality is a bit different from an aligned mind. Divinity implies something that is the finest, subtlest. The subtlest of the subtle is the state of absolute nothingness. This is Source, the space of all wisdom and highest existence. Zen Buddhism calls this "Nothingness". The more we align with this dimension, the more we naturally experience the true beauty and divinity of universal wisdom, freedom, happiness, creativity, inspiration, joy, and abundance.

"When you realize there is nothing lacking, the whole world belongs to you" - Lao Tzu.

The state of Source is true freedom, abundance, and wellbeing. It will dissolve all lower frequencies allowing growth in wisdom and joy along life's journey. The path is juicy with joy, love, meaning, and gratitude to the point that one realizes there is no lack. It is a state of perfect unity. The more the lower frequencies dissolve, the greater one's joy and bliss.

A BEAUTIFUL WORLD

Mental states have no common ground. Individuals argue because of differences, not knowing that we are living in a world of infinite possibilities. No one is right or wrong, just different levels of perception or alignment. Fighting because of differences is the biggest delusion and never ends. Fighting only stops when ego dissolves and unity/love replaces it. Love can heal the pain and war. Hate cannot. Love cares, love doesn't destroy.

When you align with the energy of truth through prayer or wisdom, you naturally attract materials like this book. In Zen Tradition, often a master says "we all have Buddha Nature", "you are already awakened, you are Buddha" These are all direct pointers to this Source that is you at the deepest level. The subtlest of all the subtle, the finest of all fine. Source is the Zero Point Field or Nirvana.

Source is the only unified field of all beings and life forces, it is the unique origin of all life forms. The more I am in alignment with Source, the more I experience life at the vibration level of all lives around me. In my heart, I can sense the vibration of a tree, the ground, crystals, animals, humans, but especially the environment because everything affects everything. This dimension of perception fascinates my mind through the synchronicities and miracles unfolding before my eyes. My life experience now is beyond comprehension of my mind, a new reality of flowing with life as source energy itself. It is fun and mysterious. I become an explorer of life itself. The adventure gets more and more interesting everyday with no time for boredom. The universe is always fresh and new in the now. Just witnessing a baby leaf or the sky is enough to vibrate all my cells with joy and ecstasy. Every moment is an opportunity to experience the vibrance of life. Babies naturally experience this dimension before they learn to speak, think, and act. That is why they are happy, loved, and cared for by universal energy manifested in human form.

As babies we were born with our true nature, fascinated with just about everything. We lived as explorers, fearlessly trusting in our true divinity. Babies never doubt their ability to walk or to run. When they fall, they get up without any doubt or fear. That is true trust. What if we, as adults, could have the mind of an explorer, and be fearless, doubtless? There are geniuses like Nikola Tesla, Albert Einstein, Steve Jobs. They all demonstrated this quality by exploring new possibilities, creativity, or inventions. Successful people act on their inner calling. In other words, when one possesses a beginner's mind, a Zen mind, we live in the world of infinite creativity. We become an inspiration to all others. We are then free from competition, criticism, imitation, or reactions we don't like. When human beings tune into their creative power, they will do exactly what they are inspired and meant to do. A life of purpose, joy, harmony, and fulfillment.

DIFFERENT MEDITATION STYLES

Direct pointer/masters first realized their true nature, then aligned it to experience life. Traditions that teach through direct pointers are Zen and other non-duality teachings. There are a variety of terms used through the ages, languages, and religions to name this unnamable: The Absolute, God, Source, Spirit, Soul, etc. They all point to this one thing, that which can't be named because language itself is not it!

Direct pointers realize their true nature or Nirvana first then practice it. There are other traditions that teach one to first purify the body & mind, moving from the grosser to subtlest vibrations and finally realizing Nirvana, the Absolute. I myself devoted two years living in Theravada Monasteries in the forests of Myanmar as a

Buddhist Nun with determination to practice the path of purification to realize Nirvana in this very life..

I realized that both paths lead to the same place: the Absolute. The Absolute is the simplest yet it is the source of clarity, universal knowledge and intelligence. I present to you both paths in which I directly practiced and realized the deepest truth behind all Buddhist traditions and Enlightened Masters at all times

.

LIFE PURPOSE AND FULFILLMENT

Two years of forest dwelling as a nun happened to be my path but it does not have to be yours. Each and every one of us is different, having unique gifts and experiences to share in this precious human lifetime. Life becomes joyful when we realize that we are deeply loved by life itself. Life is precious, and we have gifts to share. The very purpose of life is to share our gifts. The process of sharing is tremendously fulfilling. Zen masters often remind others to *find the treasure within*.

IT IS NOT ABOUT PRACTICE

My little sister has been awake since before she was 8 years old. She is awake even in deep sleep and has remained so since then. This is called super-consciousness, Nirvana, or awakened consciousness.

My meditation Masters consistently praised my speedy progress, however, when I taught my sister, it took her much less time to pass through the stages of bliss, ecstasy, oneness, ect.

Each one of you is very special. Since this book presents both sides of the same coin leading to Nirvana or Source, I can already feel that many of you will realize your true nature before completing this book.

We don't have to suffer immensely in order to realize our true nature which is the key to unlocking our purpose and fulfillment.

Often after experiencing pain, suffering, and hardship people start asking how to be happy, how to find true purpose and fulfillment. When you ask the question, the answer will always be given, because questioning leads us to the path that holds the answers.

Adept meditators know that when we are misaligned, ungrounded, imbalanced emotionally or energetically, we suffer discomfort in our body and mind. Remember, there is nothing happening to us that is outside of us. Our own consciousness creates our every body/mind experience at every moment. No one else is responsible.

"Don't let the behavior of others destroy your inner peace" - Dalai Lama.

When someone makes you unhappy, the discomfort only lives in your mind and a tense heaviness in the body. Advanced meditators can experience in their heart space the frequency of this discomfort. It is gross, dense, and not as subtle and flowing like frequencies of joy and happiness.

YOUR DIVINITY

True masters are are in charge of their thoughts, emotions, energy, and perception. They allow energies to flow through them with pure joy and at times, appreciation. It is how they transform life energy in a way it serves them and the life of others for the highest good.

Creators perceive and interpret reality the way they choose to. Indeed, that is seeing the world through the eyes of God.

A state of allowing is Zen living. Every moment is new, embraced, appreciated, and allowed with joy and ease. Source has no form and always flows with the whole. Any stagnation is caused by attachment to forms. Masters understand and operate at an energy level beyond thinking. They choose to allow and trust in the flow of wellbeing because stagnation is very dense, very far from God (heaven, your true and free nature). Masters flow as Source, the bliss of Nirvana that they are and you are originally. Masters are always connected with you at the deepest level because they know who you are. You are also Source at the absolute level, and all is one including you and them, originating from the Absolute. You can never be apart from God. God is who you are at the deepest level. When you purify what you are not, you realize your sacredness and divinity.

ATTACHMENT CAUSES STAGNATION

Energy constantly flows in a state of newness of becoming. When we hold on to something, we stagnate and life does not flow with ease, newness, and joy. When we live with thoughts of the past, life seems very old, boring, and repetitive. Indeed, life is always fresh and new in the eyes of Source and God.

WHAT IS ENLIGHTENMENT?

Infants don't operate based on memory. They are at the state of being, they are life and flow as life in the now. That is why infants are pure, happy, energetic, and lovable. They are taken care of by life, the universe works for them via their parents or loved ones. Before realization, I did not know my state when I was an infant. Now, I can always recall that state. That state is who we are beyond time and space, it is Nirvana. Enlightenment is remembering who we really are.

ATTENTION CREATES EXPERIENCE

Advanced meditators can see this very clearly. Every time we give attention to something, at that very moment, we experience it in our body/mind. We create that reality through our attention. Then the mind comes in and interprets further, based on past experience/memory. Our attention and involvement magnifies that reality in our perception (mind). The thinking mind loves to make conclusions based on past memories, however life is always in the process of changing and becoming new. When we attach and live with past memories, we live a very delayed and limited life. For example, yesterday you judged a person as miserable or negative because something that happened to them right before you met and they didn't know how to master their mind and emotions. They looked or sounded angry to you. Note that an unhappy person cannot be happy at the same time unless he or she knows how to switch their emotion by mastery or stay as Source. However, emotions are impermanent, they don't last forever. The next day you meet that person again and their emotions have changed. They might be in a neutral or happy state. When you don't perceive life with intelligence and newness of Source, you see them through the filters and conclusions of yesterday's memory which is not their current state. Enlightened people see life as it really is through the eyes of freedom. They don't miss life because they are always newly, aligned in the now. Whether the other person is angry or not, has nothing to do with the master's flow of ease.

THE CAUSE OF STRESS

When we hold on to people's emotions and accumulate those files in the mind it slows down our human computer. The mind's process doesn't stop at judging. When you think the person is bad, you naturally project that impression with gestures, thoughts, and words that reflect that belief. It is then projected on to them. If the other person doesn't know how to master their mind, they repeat the process just like you did. They might think "this person is so unhappy, rude, etc.", then all their memories of the past join them and they make conclusions about you and project that back to you through their body expression, gestures, thoughts, and speech when you both meet.

Like that the process goes on multiplying. Relationships in our time become more complicated than ever because we don't just meet one or two individuals a day.

There are constant communications and interactions in the workplace, at home, and socializing. If we are so focused on the mind's interpretation of accumulated past memories, we live a very stressful life. When we know who we really are, we also know who the others really are. Being grounded in oneness imparts compassion, wisdom/understanding, greatness, and goodwill.

TRANSCENDING LIMITATIONS

Without Mastery or knowing who we are, past memories get thicker everyday until we experience stress. The clouds of stress cover your source of clarity and wisdom. That is why when people see life through filters they seem unhappy, rigid, and less alive. The fresh and happy people can sense the compulsive thoughts when they are around unhappy vibrations because the atmosphere is very tense. When someone is so used to living in a box, they don't know there is a world outside of it. They believe the box is the only reality. This strong belief system will cause them to disagree when someone tells them of different reality. They will try to pull others into the box with them if they can because that is the only reality they know. That is why being open minded is a very important quality to growth and enjoyment of life to the fullest.

For many, at certain points in life, they start taking actions such as learning forgiveness. It is a new filter but a better one. One learns positive self-help ideas and wisdom. If one continues growing on the path of finding oneself, ultimately one realizes the whole game of playing lost just to be found.

ENLIGHTENMENT REVEALS LIFE PURPOSE AND FULFILLMENT

Only after enlightenment, can one experience true freedom, divinity, mystery, and sacredness. People realize that at the deepest level they are Source, and flow in life with universal intelligence, aligned, and intuitive. Being Source, they automatically flow through life as their purpose is revealed. Fulfillment is then joyfully experienced in the process of manifesting or creating their life. One becomes a creator of one's own reality. Eventually, one becomes a master who leads the way for others to realize themselves, their purpose and fulfillment.

MY JOURNEY OF PURIFICATION

I feel so lucky to have met and practiced under direct guidance of the best Theravada teachers of our time. After my first three months of silent retreat in the forest of Myanmar with Master U. J. he took the Sangha (ordained disciples) and other students to a small town nearby where he guided a retreat. I was a nun at that time. On the last day of the retreat he gave his last Dhamma talk in front of Sangha and all others practitioners in the town. Right after his talk, he asked me to give a Dhamma talk for ten minutes because he was amazed by my speedy progess, insights, and realizations of the truth. Many times he recommended me to become a meditation teacher.

I once met a female teacher in UBaKhin, a meditation center where master Goenka himself graduated. She was one of his classmates. After many tests she confirmed that I had reached Nirvana. I share these experiences so that you understand where I am coming from and allow me to help you the way I was helped. The only way for me to give back all the blessings that I received from my masters is to spread the truth that has set me free. I know it will also set you free because the truth is always with you on your path. [5]

DIFFERENT LEVELS OF MASTERY

In addition to my enlightened Theravada masters, I was blessed to have met other enlightened Zen masters in my search. I had set my intention very clearly to meet and practice with enlightened masters who could show me how to achieve the same freedom. I manifested exactly that - enlightened masters.

At least two of my Zen masters are already free from the cycle of birth and death, meaning they can choose to consciously die or prolong their lives. This is true mastery. I want to share that possibility with the world at this time. Any conscious creator in their journey will gain more mastery and wisdom as life goes. Life just gets more and more fruitful. You can consciously design your reality including birth and death.

Four and a half years ago in 2015 while reading Akashic records, both masters told me that I would reach my mature state in four more years. Two years after that, a Theravada master in Myanmar told me that it will take me another two years. Note that all three of them from different places in the world gave me the exact time frame that it would take me to reach full realization. Their prediction came true.

Within those four years I saw subatomic particles in space and was able to hear the cosmic Om sound at any time. I was also developing just like they were during their earlier journey to enlightenment. That is why they call this the Path. It can take no time to realize one's true nature, but it takes time for maturity in mastery, and skills to share this gift.

After about four years time, I came across Mooji Papa's teaching and read the book *The Power of Now* by Eckhart Tolle. Before this point I only knew how to enter the absolute state in sitting meditation. I had kept the book *The Power of Now* with me during the past seven years but never completed until the exact time I needed it most. When I read that book, tears came to my eyes. I realized that these masters, in different ways, reached the Absolute. It took me the whole path of purification to realize it. But I did not know how to incorporate it in daily life. These masters knew how.

Along my journey, I receive answers that take me to higher states of wisdom. My Masters, especially Mooji Papa, out of compassion, points others directly to Nirvana without intense practice. This realization can be applied in daily activities. Theravada teaches meditators to experience Nirvana during sitting meditation in seclusion. Each technique is actually half of the picture. It is best to know both parts because they support, not conflict with one another. It is beneficial to be able to incorporate Nirvana in daily life. On the other hand, when people are given direct pointers so easily, they tend to not value them as much. I myself experienced the Absolute through a long and intensive path of purification which not many people in our modern society have the opportunity to follow. I had to pass through all stages of insights and different levels of euphoric bliss in order to realize and appreciate the divinity and power of the Absolute. There are a few times students realized this Absolute through my direct pointing. They experienced it but just keep going back to their mental games, not allowing Source to take over and reveal the secrets of enlightenment. They believed more in their mental noise because it is more tangible compared with the Absolute. A lot of times, the human mind needs to pass through the whole game in order to know what is best.

Bliss and euphoria feel good but are not the end game. These states are impermanent. When we find the permanence, the source of who we are, we can get the most out of life. Bliss and euphoria come after enlightenment and intensify over time. Otherwise we are constantly fluctuationing until we are secure in the permanence of Nirvana. The Zero point. The real deal.

SAGES ARE THE WILDEST

The enlightened are religious masters so you don't often get to see their wild side. They enjoy life more than our minds can comprehend. When I listen to music, the cells in my body vibrate ecstatically. My orgasm becomes an orgasm of each and every cell. A baby leaf can make my whole body vibrate with joy and appreciation. Enlightened people enjoy life to its fullest and wildest. They are blissful at the cellular level. It does not require a party or drugs to feel happy. Their orgasmic bliss can be triggered easily at cellular level. The intensity is beyond comprehension. The normal mind is very gross compared with life experienced at the cellular level. The enlightened live an orgasmic life. It is difficult to explain this using words, but I can because I already freed myself from religion. Truth is the goal of all religions, it is never the other way around. Enlightenment is experiential.

THE BENEFITS OF CONTINUOUS PRACTICE

The untrained mind is normally restless, scattered, and therefore too gross to perceive the deepest truths. The average ten days retreat is recommended because continuous mindfulness is powerful. It sharpens awareness to higher dimensions of consciousness. The refined or calmed mind can experience higher frequencies of bliss, tranquility, equanimity, compassion, wisdom, and finally Nirvana.

BREATH AWARENESS

I can't stress enough the importance of this technique. Breath is one of the most powerful tools for mastery. Any path of purification that involves mindfulness of breath is indeed wise because breath helps us attain enlightenment with ease and joy along the way. I witnessed at least two people attain realization of Nirvana only through mindfulness on the breath within a one month retreat because I was their interpreter. Breath is Prana or life force and has a form. I saw Prana myself both with closed and open eyes while being mindful of the breath in my first ten days of Goenka Vipassana retreat. Later when I heard one of my masters describe it, I recognized that he also saw it. Through my closed eyes I saw Prana as pure, beautiful white, strong, wide, powerful and long. Through my open eyes it was divine, subtle, long, pure white particles.

Any mind that is calm and concentrated through continuous mindfulness on the breath can perceive reality at these higher dimensions. It is relatively easy and pleasant to practice mindfulness on the breath. I experienced so many blissful tears of peace and joy in my earlier journey. Now I often experience tears of joy and bliss in deeper meditation on the wisdom of understanding, realizations, and appreciation of life experiences or new unfolding. This path is beautiful.

Breath itself has a form and so do thoughts. One of my masters can see auras and thoughts of people in his daily life. I adore him for his level of continuous concentration. In retreats I joined, many friends in awakened states said that they, at times, perceived reality at celestial levels. They described surroundings as crystalline and can see things great distances. Life forms were extraordinarily pleasant, divine, and beautiful beyond any human treasures. These types of experiences are familiar to me because I myself experienced them and witnessed fellow meditators experience them on a regular basis just because the environments I chose to be in. For some who are familiar with these realities, it makes total sense because the environments and people one surrounds oneself with everyday shape one's perception and belief system. Belief system or possibility of a person does not mean that it is the possibility of this universe. We all grow and learn new things everyday, even scientists. The fact is that people with talents and special abilities are being discovered and shared more and more on TV and YouTube channels everyday. This universe has infinite possibilities and the more open we are to learn, experience, and create new possibilities, the more we allow new and infinite potential show up in our life.

Life is joyous and we are meant to experience beauty, greatness, and inspiration. It can be an adventurous, fulfilled life untill the time of departure. We will come back to Source, our oneness with the nature of purity and freedom. These were reported by many scientists in our time through hundreds if not thousands of cases of near death experience and I myself realized the deathlessness along with many other near and dear ones. While we are here in human form, let's discover and experience life to the highest and fullest. Buddha himself told his disciples to not believe in what he says. He encouraged them to try what he teaches and experience the same truth for themselves. They need to see reality at higher dimensions and witness others around them also experience these miracles on a regular basis. Then their belief system upgrades to new possibilities which always exist in the universe, ready to be discovered.

Mindfulness on breath helps one be distracted from resistance or unpleasant energies of both body and mind and easily achieve states of joy, tranquility, and ecstasy. Once one experiences the benefits, one naturally has the motivation and personal experience to continue and open more doors on the path to Nirvana.

The technique is simple and natural. Just be mindful of the breath continuously especially before and after sleep. This way one sleeps in a very productive meditative mode. Maybe soon your sleep will be like my sister's, a conscious sleep. Mindfulness on the breath does not require sitting posture, it is best when your body is comfortable, cozy, and at ease. Just be with the breath as much as you can even when you fall asleep. While observing, your sleep is more meditative. You can check by measuring brainwaves and see the difference. With continuous practice, after a few days, it forms a new habit.

When the mind has an object to be aware of, it does not waste energy repeating compulsive thoughts. Clarity of mind is important and focus on the breath is one of the best tools I know to attain it. I can flow in life as Source but mindfulness of breath is even more powerful and helps us protect our energy better especially when it comes to manifesting. I notice every time I practice mindfulness on the breath, everything is effortlessly taken care of for me. Breath is Source power, life energy that flows through everything. When we tune into that frequency of wellbeing, everything works out for our highest good. It is recommended to dedicate a few days doing breath work in nature or in a peaceful environment because other people can affect one another energetically. When you are mindful or connected you will start realizing that other's mind energy is not yours! For beginners, let's keep it simple by first finding a place that is suitable for meditation. When more advanced, you can start exploring the energy and thoughts of others and see how everything is connected. Group sitting is wonderful because mindfulness of groups is very powerful and can help you concentrate easier. I highly recommend the Goenka ten-day course. There are centers around the globe. The people are loving, and the energy is amazing. Make sure you complete the full ten day course to receive the maximum benefit.

Mindfulness becomes automatic and effortless after a few days of continuous practice, and one will start experiencing the joy, happiness, and wellbeing in the body mind. This investment is worth everything in the universe. Outer manifestation of joy, abundance, harmony, etc., are just side benefits of one's inner state of alignment, joy and wellbeing. Things that match your vibration of love, joy, wellbeing, abundance will start flowing into your reality.

My master also taught me how to expand my consciousness and told me to help others the way she did for me. Teaching bring us peace, freedom, and wisdom.

Energy constantly flows and is the key. My body/mind during such periods was like a flute of divinity, so peaceful and joyful. Now I know when energy flows without any doubt or stagnation or confusion. Our true nature flows blissfully in pure energy. Low frequencies such as confusion or doubt are very dense and create stagnation or discomfort in our energy field. That is why enlightened masters always teach about detachment, ridding ourselves of the dense and limiting belief systems to allow pure energy to flow.

MULTI-DIMENSION

We are living in a divine multi-dimensional universe, experience the world through our individual perceptions. The more concentrated and calm the mind is, the more beautiful the universe gets because one perceives the world through their current state of being. Advance meditators can see this clearly.

I experienced many times, especially in meditation retreats, a universe alive and vibrant with purity of love, joy, and magnificent intelligence. I also experience these states when I am in nature or alone without electrical devices. Nature is always in a state of being with pure joy and peace. Many people recently told me that they realized they are happier when they are in nature.

Nature does not generate anger, fear, guilt, and other dense frequencies, only the human mind can. However, the human mind also has the capacity to generate high frequencies of love, appreciation, and all other ones that are pleasant to be around. It is not hard, only the awareness to know oneself, the true nature of being that is peaceful and joyous. By not knowing ourselves or true nature, one takes oneself to be the fleeting mental states which are rootless in nature. If we base our life on something that is rootless and fluctuates, we live a life of imbalance or being ungrounded. If we realize who we really are we start experiencing the unfolding of higher frequencies of love, harmony, good will, creativity, joy, etc. The fruits just keep getting sweeter and sweeter. It is the sweetness of divinity.

TRANSCEND SADNESS AND RAISE FREQUENCY

The irritated mind is unpleasant to be around for it is quite low frequency compared with our true origin. We are pure in nature, that is why we can perceive something that is grosser or lower vibration. Just like when one is more conscious, we can recognize those who are less conscious or not mindful. Many times I can perceive the irritated mind of family members downstairs when they first wake up and before they even start making any sounds. Those who master their mind, they wake up mindfully, with joy, and gratitude. They direct thoughts in a positive direction. Those not in charge of their mind, go to sleep with mental noise and overwhelming or irritating thoughts and emotions. They wake up with sadness, fear, grief, anger, etc., which sets the vibrational tone for their day. They keep on attracting the frequencies they give focus to and see the world through that filter of low frequency/emotion. A life like that is a punishment.

Many years ago, I was the same, I woke up with grief and sadness because I was treated with jealousy and hatred by a classmate who also wanted others to dislike me. Every morning I woke up feeling bad and not wanting to go to school. I did not know how to overcome that daily sadness. Everyday I kept going to school giving attention to those classmates and their negative behaviors, I did not know that I could actually use that same time to focus on pleasant experiences such as gratitude for the good friends or to learn from those who are inspiring and positive.

I busied myself focusing on the negativity of others and woke up every morning feeling bad and wanted to hide from the world. Many years later, after learning meditation and understanding how the body and mind works, I realized that what other people do has nothing to do with me. It is the journey they choose to experience. It is how I choose to experience my life that matters. Intelligent people interpret things the way they choose to. When a person brings a gift to us and we don't accept it, that person must take it home. It's the same with people's behavior. When they are positive, happy and joyful to be around, we can join in. If they are negative and drain our energy because they don't know how to master their happiness, we can either help them if they are willing to be helped, and if not, we can choose to spend time with happy frequencies that resonate with our highest good. When we let our vibration get dragged down, we become a victim of the game. The only thing that one can get from people of low frequencies is anger, complaining, guilt, shame, hatred, etc. It is very important to raise our frequency by mind mastery, only then we can offer help to others around us.

When we walk on the path of alignment which is realigning with who we really are, we get to experience the truer dimensions of joy, love, bliss, aliveness and intelligence of the universe. Humans often focus on problems like negativity, fear, and doubt that spreads like a flu. The biggest flu-like disease to me is the way many people use their mind, not as a master but as a victim.

Masters are those who take back their authority by using the mind to create their highest and most joyful life experiences. All of us have that ability. When more and more of us become masters of our reality, the frequency of the universe changes. Love and wellbeing then become the prominent frequencies in the world. Just like anything we choose to learn in life, we can learn meditation and become masters of our reality. Based on my experience, I can tell you that investment in meditation is worth more than all other investments I can make for myself. One can learn to become a doctor, lawyer, school teacher, etc. But by learning to master one's mind, one masters the rest of their experience for everything will be led by the intelligence of Source. Decisions will then be driven based on happiness, passion, inspiration instead of fear, doubt, anger, hatred, jealousy, or resentment. Abundance is then just a side effect of doing what we love and are inspired to do.

THE SHADOW WORK

After connecting me with the breathing practice, my master then proceeded to explain shadow work as a way to purify dense and outdated belief systems. This technique helped me dissolve the hidden subconscious memories that caused me pain, regret, and suffering. My Master asked me to remember the events that made me suffer with pain, guilt, shame, etc. She guided me to look at each event one by one objectively with my awareness/ observing mind while naturally allowing my breath.

At first I remember the event that caused deep guilt and shame when I was a teenager. I used insulting words and caused my mom to cry. When I relived that memory, the emotions of shame and guilt came and I sobbed. After seeing myself released from that emotion of guilt, my master then guided me to look at that same event one more time consciously while breathing. This time I noticed the emotion was reduced. I was no longer crying because the denser energy of ego transformed to higher frequency under the light of pure consciousness. Energy is always in the process of becoming or transforming. Then just to make sure the energy was totally transformed, she asked me to relive that event one more time. This time it was rather hard to see the event clearly but I noticed I was able to look at the event objectively without emotion attached to it. It was like watching a movie outside of myself. It flowed without any dense emotions left. That was when my master knew the energy was completely transformed. I repeated the process for all other events that caused negative emotions. I get better when using this technique with other emotional events, because each time I can view events objectively with little or no emotion attached right after the first attempt. Only through personal experience, I know this technique works, it is called reprogramming the subconscious mind. Whatever we give energy to, grows or magnifies. In this case, we give energy to observing the clear mind, not to false mental states or ego. Gross energies are transformed to pure consciousness.

The first session of shadow work was about 20 minutes and my frequency raised to a totally different person, not just a shift in vibration. The body is also vibration and connects closely with any shift in mind or consciousness. Following this my face became noticeably brighter and prettier. I felt very light and joyful. My master is the most skillful person I know.

REALIZING THE COSMIC SOUND

After shadow work, the master asked us to do group sitting meditation for a few minutes while she expanded her consciousness. She then asked if we noticed a sound that is subtle and not created by man or anything else. There was one friend that heard it, and asked the other two of us to cover our ears and notice that sound. I was able to hear it and described it to her as an high tone, cricket-like buzzing sound but continuous and subtle. She confirmed that it was correct. This sound once connected is for good forever. One can always hear it at any time. When this sound is present, one is in the state of pure awareness, only the knower or Source knows this sound. I remembered hearing this sound when I was in danger as a teenager but not knowing what it was.

My father's business was boat building so he stored many large pieces of wood near the sea shore. My brother and cousin knew how to swim and often hungout there. I did not know how to swim properly at that time so was warned not to play in that area because there are some deep spots in the ocean that cannot be seen. Part of my natural curiosity leads me to do exactly what I am told not to. One afternoon while playing on the floating wood, I put my feet in the water and noticed that I could touch the bottom. I then started to practice swimming, and really had fun doing so, completely forgetting the warning. I was swimming and at the point when trying to stand I found there was no ground under me. While drowning however, I was in a state of pure being, no fear at all. I remember so clearly that moment the OM sound became prominent, I was at peace with what is. I can recall it right now. After that, I received a push from somewhere and before I noticed anything, I was next to and grappling a big floating log. I was a kid and at the point of drowning I had no fear, only peace and total state of allowing. I was taken care by life force itself in the form of my brother. He was 15 years old, saw me drowning, and was intelligent enough to know that if he grabbed me attempting to save me I might drag him down drowning both of us. He decided to push me from a distance with his "kung fu" leg and that moved me to the floating log. I have watched many near death experience videos shared by doctors or neuroscientists, noticing one thing in common. The victum can always recall the near death experience at anytime for it is more real than any other experience in ones mind. It is so true in my case. It taught me the difference between spirit/instinct and thinking. I can always recall moments of peace and the absolute because truth always exists and is who we really are. Who we really are always exists, is always here and now. We can forget who we are not easily, but once we recognize who we really are, it becomes imprinted or enlightened.

Now think about the moment you first put your hand near fire and the instinct that automatically pulled your hand away from danger. You cannot forget the intensity of the burn or the pain because that belongs to perception. Often, the mind remembers what fear and pain really are. The mind is good at conceptualizing what happens. Instinct is pure/intelligent protection and always leads you in the most beautiful and spontaneous way. These days humans use a fancier word - intuition. That is a beautiful word.

When the body needs energy, it sends the signal of hunger, same with thirst, and toilet needs. It needs no comprehension of the mind. The mind jumps in and decides what to eat. Do I want fish, or meat, or tofu? What should I drink? Soda, juice, or water. But when it comes to the toilet, the mind can think whatever it wants but the body intelligence will push out whatever amount that needs to be released from our body to keep us going. Unless we abuse the body to the level that it shuts down, it is always doing its best to sustain our life. When we eat, the body sends the signal when we are full. For advanced meditators, myself included, in intensive meditation retreats, when I eat mindfully, I can sense the vibration of the food in my body. When you are mindful enough, everything is vibration and a pure and sharpened mind can perceive reality as vibrating particles. These particles can also be seen with open or closed eyes. A lot of times people don't live at the level of vibration because the mind is gross or clouded by compulsive thoughts. They only believe in what science & advanced devices tell them. The good news is, as science discovers more about consciousness, mind and matter, many scientists are taking their research to meditation centers like in Myanmar.

When one can't sense the vibration of the food, one may eat things that are unhealthy for the body. However, as I always send love and appreciation to my foods prior to consumption, I also eat mindfully, every mouthfull vibrates in my stomach and transforms to pure energy. I notice that when I eat food that is organic and healthy, the effects of those vibrations serve my vitality better. Those who are mindful can sense the vibration of food and can tell if it is made with love, joy, and good intentions. Foods vibrate at a high frequency and are noticeable to a mindful individual. One time I had lunch with my soulmate at a macrobiotic place in Ho Chi Minh City, Vietnam. Every food that came from that kitchen had a very high frequency. Both of us noticed the difference when compared with other restaurants we ate at those days. That was a very delightful experience.

Foods that are high frequency are one thing, the other thing is collective energy. Normally people who eat macrobiotics are very mindful, grateful toward their food, and chew well. We were connecting with the collective peaceful energy of the food and the mindful people who came before us. The energy didn't die. Mindful vibrations remain in the room. With a bit of awareness, we can sense the energies at different places. Let's say when you go to a supermarket, how do you feel? When in nature how do you feel? And when you go to a meditation center, how do you feel? Those who are adept in vibration can sense or see the particles at a meditation center vibrate at a very high frequency. When we sit down and meditate it is so easy to enter high states of peace and happiness compared with meditating at home or in a public place. In peaceful environments, particles and the Om sound are most prominent.

I had a conversation with two friends who are very advanced spiritually. One can see different dimensions beyond time and space. The other attained enlightenment as a child. Our conversation was delightful and other worldly. Two of us (Nhan & I) were testing Liem, the one with the ability to see beyond time and space. Liem did not know English nor have access to new age groups or techniques. Nhan knows how to connect others with higher self (or spirit). After he helped Liem connect with his higher self, Liem had the ability to see anywhere he wants and can answer any question. Our conversations were about that, Nhan and I taking advantage of this little brother's ability. His answers were all confirmed by reports of Dolores Cannon and other famous new age individuals. We asked him to tell us what happened on the moon, what the matrix looks like, my aura, my master's aura, etc. His answers matched what we heard from new age leaders in the west.

Nhan connected me with my spiritual guide. At this point I only knew Zen meditation, not much about new age spirituality until he told me. I suddenly realized the desire to connect with my higher self, the cosmic intelligence to help me navigate life experiences in the most ecstatic way. It was important because I didn't want to just live in peace and wait for a peaceful death. I choose to live an enlightened and extraordinary life before conscious departure.

Who says we can't have both. Some traditions think that wanting superpowers is egotistical. The truth is, Buddha himself had superpowers. Whether or not he used them, we don't know. What if labeling superpowers as "egotistical" was somehow added to Buddhist teachings at some later date to keep them from future Buddhist, thus limiting them to a less powerful state. Conscious/pure people with superpower will use them for the highest good of all. What if you had abundance to eradicate poverty, to support poor meditators, to retire your parents, be generous with your friends. Even if you had more money than you ever needed/wanted, wouldn't it be nice to manifest your ideal romantic, supportive, and enlightened relationships in this lifetime? Is it nice to manifest an ecstatic energetic body? What if we could live an enlightened and prosperous life in all areas. What if we could live an enlightened life and manifest the celestial? Celestial is beyond a human dimension, yet has the same true nature that is source. What if we could experience a life that is beneficial to ourselves and the surroundings toward wellbeing, joy, happiness, freedom, and sovereignty?

I don't believe in limitation and boundary. I believe in infinite possibilities, even those that have yet to be discovered and shared. Nirvana itself is infinite, it can give birth to anything. There will be more teachings that are not just about enlightenment but how to live the enlightened life of our dreams. As Nhan connected me with my spiritual guide, he directed me to ask my spiritual guide what dimension I am from. I saw numbers 8 and 9 clearly in my mind. I was doubting, not sure what "dimension" means and what "8 and 9" meant. At that time, Nhan said, "I told you earlier, you belongs to Quanyin dimension, which is dimension 8 and 9." I still did not believe in this until after a few more incidents occurred when the three of us met and talked.

One time the walls were vibrating, almost liquid-like and all three of us saw it. At times, the time-space stopped and all three of us experienced it. I secretly called my spiritual guide and at the same time Liem, the one who can see dimensions, screamed "it's so bright, someone just came to Tammie." As I walk this path of conscious, mysteries start unfolding in my life and open doors of infinite possibilities, creativity, and joy. This path of enlightenment is fun and never limited as we are told from time to time. Anything that is a limitation is dense in frequency and is not who we are. As creators, we can create infinite possibilities because everything is energy created through awareness and source intelligence. It is a journey, make it fun on your path of discovery. This path is miraculous, we were already miraculous before we took this physical form, we are just playing the game of remembering and appreciating our awesomeness.

MEDITATION AND HEALING POWER

When one tunes in with the vibration of the body, one knows exactly what to do every moment. Advanced meditators rarely get sick because when small, dense vibration are noticed, they use their power of mindfulness to eradicate them quickly. They don't get to the point where to much dense energy/illness accumulates. Their pure consciousness (energy) constantly purifies dense energy or we may say, they stay at the level beyond the body. They align with pure consciousness, they don't stay as the body so they are not affected by the body dimension.

Every morning, I wake up with dense energy in the neck and head, because I normally align my energy to the state of flow. When some very tiny density lingers in my body's cells, I sit and meditate. This dissolve them and my body returns to the state of flow again. Often people live in a world where everyone seems in a hurry going somewhere and doing something, like running away from themselves. They accumulated too much ungrounded energies like worry and fear. As their day goes on, they attract similar vibrations from others and end up storing anger, hatred, guilt, and other dense vibrations in their body/energy field. Overtime energy can't flow if one constantly lives in a state of resistance or being ungrounded. Those energies become one's normal life or prominent frequency and belief system. They no longer believe life is good, that pain, and sickness are normal. Some wait to the point when a doctor says "I am sorry, I can't..." before starting to love themselves, going into nature, going inward or find other ways of healing. In meditation retreats, first time meditators often report much pain and unhealed trauma surfacing from childhood. But as they continue witnessing it, their mindfulness neutralizes the trauma or dense energies, eradicating them one by one. Their faces are radiant once again, they all become happier. The retreat changed their life for the better. They learned how to transform their emotional pain through the power of mindfulness. There is a whole book in Mahashi Sayadaw Meditation Method under Theravada Buddhism in Myanmar of accounts of people healed from chronic diseases that medical doctors said "sorry, I already tried my best…". Many cases experienced tumors bursting energetically during meditation. Returning their doctors found the tumors had completely disappeared. Tumor is indeed an accumulated energy of pain and dense belief. Just like the water experiment has proven, when you keep absorbing negative energies, the fluid cells turn abnormally ugly and distorted.

First reading the meditation reports of others, I was not convinced they were true. Later during my own meditation I experienced pains vanishing. Only then was I convinced of the healing power of meditation. I would encourage you to try and see for yourself the benefit of meditation in balancing all life areas because it helps us get back into the vortex, the pure positive energy and infinite potential that we really are originally.

JOY, OUR NATURAL STATE

What if I told you that joy is your natural state. That is the very thing people keep telling me so often especially at meditation centers where people recognize, encourage, and value happiness. They tell me that I look so happy.

When the body/mind is tranquil, there is pure joy and bliss. We cannot expect hatred or anger to come out from a person while he or she is happy. Similarly, when a person is angry or overwhelmed, we cannot expect peace and bliss to come from them. When the inner energy flows, one moves in life with ease and joy, faces glow and can't help but radiate their inner joy and happiness. They look younger than their age. People always tell me that I look like a teenager or in my twenties. I witnessed many of my meditator friends who are in their seventies look like they are in their forties. Everything is vibration. When people vibrate at the purest level, they radiate symmetrical crystalline at the cellular level of aliveness. Body form is nothing but a combination of cells. Their cells vibrate at the ultimate level to keep them happy and healthy. There are numerous scientific reports on the hormones or natural chemicals that are released from the body-mind in the meditating brain waves such as serotonin, endorphins, etc., to keep people looking younger and happier.

Body pain is a sign of accumulated dense energy caused by ones belief system. When you are unconscious of your true nature, you accept it by learning from others around you who often are also unconscious of their true nature. A stressful society is a group of ungrounded people not knowing who they truly are and spreading the disease of ungroundedness. Life seems like a battle for those who are ungrounded or imbalanced. They have to work very hard to earn very little. Happy, positive people are those who are passionate in what they do or do the job that makes them happy. They tend to get the most from life. Steve Jobs, Bill Gates, Jeff Bezo, singers, movie stars, etc. Everything that we put out to the Universe always returns to us. The more people you can inspire to better their lives, the more abundantly society pays you back in return for your greatness, creativity, innovation, and inspiration.

As I write this book, I clearly see that I am growing more than ever with it. It expands my wisdom and joy on a daily basis. I allow the universal intelligence to flow through me and serve the whole. Before the book is even published, I have received so many benefits even beyond the joy of writing it. I make YouTube videos because I am inspired to do so. I find myself growing and expanding in the topics I share with others. The effect is immediate. Every time I post new videos, my mind has doubts about whether audiences will like this video and whether or not I present well in the video. However, my intuition knows very well that my body/mind is just a vessel for universal intelligence, a channel to flow through. I trust in Source and it's divinity 100%. Many of my viewers receive energy and benefits from the videos. Collective energy is amazing. A few days after posting my videos, I normally watch them again. Without fail, after hundreds of visits, the energy of the video grows in power as if the viewers contribute power and positive energies to the videos which I made with love and joy.

Wisdom is very different than smartness. Wisdom is a spontaneous flow of energy wanting to express its being. I feel a sense of fulfillment since aligning myself with this flow. Smartness is about thinking which is always about the duality of good/bad, right/wrong, etc. Thinking causes confusion and is very slow and limited compared with wisdom or intuition. A true Zen master always flows through life with intuition, living by the intelligence that drives life force. He/she is always spontaneous and perfectly synchronizes with the whole. For example, nature harmoniously blends together. When a wind passes by, the leaves move in perfect harmony without resistance. I noticed many times when I talk with others on the phone, especially when it is about truth/Dhamma, I notice that their intention affects my flow of conversation. For example, when they get distracted or become uninterested, my talking stops. And when they have interest or want to know more, the Dhamma/truth just flows through me in accordance with their thoughts or intention. A few times my friend tested me by switching off and on his thought and my conversation adjusted simultaneously. A Zen mind is always in the now and blends with life without any delay. It is true beauty.

Since I flow in life like that, the secret of energy and oneness starts revealing itself in a bigger and more complete picture everyday. Beliefs are always based on memory of the past. It is not the newness or real time intelligence of the now. That is why many people lose passion for life, feeling unfulfilled, and lacking of purpose. In a way they are being limited by compulsive thoughts like clouds that cover the sky of freshness and pure intelligence. Its like stress and overwhelming mental states that cover the space of inspiration and creativity.

Life purpose is the universal purpose that manifests through an individual when one is in alignment with Source. That is how purpose and passion reveals itself. Your master does not have the same unique purpose and gifts that you do. You are the only one that can discover that for your life. Masters can only point you to the master within yourself, the Source intelligence has answers to all your questions.

The difference between the Master and others is that masters align with true nature and function based on pure intelligence. Others often believe themselves to be the "cloud" of emotions based on past experience and act upon these limited beliefs. That way, one cannot experience the infinite freedom, bliss, joy, and truth that we are. They function in the dimension of duality and not oneness or Nirvana.

HEALING POWER OF TREES

Recently I discovered a new technique about the healing power of trees, especially big ones because they are deeply rooted, connected to mother nature. Nature always vibrates at the purest vibration. Many adept meditators can see or feel this. Many times I experience the purest vibration of all forms in my meditation retreats. Humans have the special ability to experience life at multi-dimensional levels from concept or thinking to being and Source, the origin of all life.

Depending on connectedness within, one can experience different dimensions through different levels of alignment. Meditation is a tool to sharpen awareness, returning us to the true origin of pure knowingness that we were before adopting and accepting belief systems. Often people in modern society perceive life through filters of knowledge. Some are highly educated and communicate with different styles of filters compared with those who don't have much educational background. Society divides others through these filters as well. However, there is a common ground for all beings, the dimension of intuition. When everyone aligns with this intelligence, conversations flow with wisdom instead of conflict, business grows with creativity, inspiration, and passion instead of stress and competition.

A friend of mine, Daniel, is very connected with nature. When we talk, conversations flow with joy. New wisdom is being downloaded and communicated with open hearts. A person with an open heart is the nature's source of creativity, inspiration, and infinite expansion. People with closed hearts or minds limit themselves from growth, participation with the newness, infinite joy, and discovery of life.

Let's continue the story of big trees and their healing power. Those who don't have meditation experience can do research using special tools to measure nature's vibrations that I am about to share. I share based on my direct experience with vibration, as I can sense them inside my body in any location. I can also sense vibrations outside easily especially when I touch trees. Nature is always in the state of being, especially trees. There is no rite or ritual about this. I met Daniel at a meditation center. He is adept at connecting with nature. I point to the Source and he experienced it within ten minutes. In his case, he became enlightened years ago. After that, he was attracted to spirituality and meditation by his inner guidance. His higher self in celestial forms connects to guide him. He has the ability to see the energy of a person in front of him. He can see if that person is in the state of flow with ease or if they have some dense energy or stagnation in a particular area of the body. Every time we talk, his body vibrates at a very high frequency. He is not the only one. Myself and many around me experience a vibration of joy in the body when we hear truth, our cells are that intelligent. When it connects with truth which is high in frequency, it emits joyful vibrations. He told me that often he sees pain in other people's bodies but my body has none, my eyes are crystal clear with purity. He is not the only one who confirms that I am on the right path. Many masters of mine who can see auras and read Akashic records have told me about my light and the high frequency I emited even at the time when I had no clue about meditation. Note that because of the confidence I received from those who can see me beyond the human mind, I gained the confidence to go all in and dedicated years in Buddhist countries to find the truth I have found.

When I touched my palms to the tree barefooted, I noticed a tingling vibration of pain in my neck automatically vanished and I experienced wholeness again. That is when I knew trees have healing power because their roots are deep in Mother Earth. Try it for yourself. Those who can feel vibrations of the body will recognize this truth more immediately.

THE POWER OF MIND/INTENTION

One of my recent discoveries on this path is the power of intention. The other day while walking with Daniel in very cold weather, I mumbled inside, "I am warm, I am warm, I am warm," and I experienced the warmness immediately. Intention is very powerful for it is also vibration or energy generated through source intelligence. This is a process that creators realize along their journey with more and more clarity and proof. In one meditation course, there was two hours of sitting without moving the legs. I just knew somehow it was meant for higher wisdom and intelligence to come through. At the point of intense discomfort in legs and body, I stayed grounded as the knower, and decided to chant inside "I am love, I am beautiful, I am abundance." Suddenly the vibrations in my body changed from pain to pleasant.

We do have the ability to change our vibration especially in moments of challenge because at such moments, the mind does not have time to wander here and there. So recalling Dr. Emoto's water consciousness research and my own direct experience, we can see our ability to change reality at the cellular level.

ELECTROMAGNETIC FREQUENCY AND MASTERY

Nature as trees, earth, and animals have frequency of being. Electrical devices also have their own frequencies. I can sense electromagnetic frequency in my heart space. Electromagnetic frequency is grosser than that of nature and space. It is due to the collective energy of modern society. Do you notice that every time we use the phone, or computer, we tend to type fast, search fast to get things done? People use technology for work and communication. The tense energy when connected with electromagnetic frequency is strong because many people are not being mindful while using those devices. When doing business or searching for something humans are often in states of stress while using these technologies whether they are aware of it or not. We are all already psychic, it is our natural state. Do you notice when you go to an environment where people are violent, you can sense the tense energy in that area before actually seeing evidence of it? It is called intuition or knowingness. When you go to a place where people generate goodwill, love, and compassion, you can sense the energy even before anyone speaks.

When we see a child with a fearful expression, we can sense what has happened to the child in the past, punished by parents or teachers or what ever. When we see a confident, happy, creative, child we say, "your parents raised you well," even without seeing the parents. We can tell how they were treated by looking at their current behaviors. In my case, I clearly see evidence that everything has memory. Daniel gave me a crystal that he got from Mt Shasta. Holding it, I receive the energy that is grounded, content in the middle and radiating light and aura on the outside. I perceive that with closed eyes while holding it. I told him about it and he was surprised because he charged this crystal under the sun very often. The discovery was fascinating but I had no term for it until recently. I read a book called "Master in The New Energy" by Adamus Saint-Germain. The author mentioned that rocks actually have memory of everything that has ever come into contact with it. I may not have believed this if I read it before my direct experience. However, in this case, I experience reality at cosmic memory level and I attract those who hold knowledge of this into my reality. I had been vegetarian for five years, however recently, while socializing, I ate a piece of steak. That night, I experienced the consciousness of that animal. I saw its surroundings, however, there was no fear in the dream. It was just pure knowing and consciousness. There was no nightmare until I woke up and the mind tried to interpret it in terms of good or bad. Indeed, consciousness memory is just pure experience and it is fascinating to discover.

THE SURROUNDING ENVIRONMENT

The mind has a very specific frequency. I noticed this once while sleeping upstairs with my aunty downstairs. At the moment she woke up, before speaking or doing anything, I already sense her compulsive irritable thoughts. A few days later, talking with her, I was told that she changed her job and her new workplace was treating her badly. No wonder she woke up with such energy. For those who are awakened, they often like to be in nature for nature does not generate lower frequencies such as irritation, anger, stress, etc. There are people who make noise but in a good state of being and it is better than those who don't make noise but inside are so irritated. This is how I connect with life now, at the energy level. It is important for beginners to have personal time in nature or alone, especially when feeling a need to look for life purpose, discover passion, or reach fulfillment. Love yourself and give yourself a retreat. When you are out in the world, there are so much noise that you don't really know which one is yours. When you are in seclusion, you will understand yourself better. It is great if you can take a Goenka ten day meditation retreat course because at such places, people have good intentions toward others and the technique is a great tool for beginners to dive deep inside. Once you understand how body/mind mechanisms work, then you can be in the world happily. Once you can master your mind, emotion, and energy, you will attract others who hold the key to a higher level of evolution that matchs with who you are. Consciousness evolution never stops, life is always vibrant. It is fun to learn the art of living. Life is consciously discovered and enjoyed as the master, the creator that we came forth to be. Remember living a joyful, fulfilling and connected life is the purpose of every human being. Once you understand yourself, you understand the world. Once you know the origin of yourself, you know the origin of the world. Then life becomes a mysteriously fun adventure.

HEALING POWER OF HANDS AND SELF-LOVE

Every time I experience dense electromagnetic frequency in my heart space, I put my hand there. Immediately the turbulence stops. That is how I know reiki is real. Our hands have a special power especially along with the intention to heal. It works for me every time. When any part of my body has pain, I put my hand there and the pain dissolves. The body needs our love and attention so don't be afraid to hug yourself every day and watch relationships around you transform. The way people treat us is a reflection of how we treat ourselves. We see the world inside out through our filter of perception. Be at ease with yourself, learn to love yourself, inspire yourself to live a life of joy, happiness, and fulfillment. Ask the questions and the answers will come when you are in the state of allowing them. Like when you are in nature or meditation retreat where you are aligned with your natural state. That state of clarity is the treasure that all the wise talk about. When the mind is full of duality, there is no space for love, connectedness, passion, and inspiration. Just be connected with your true nature, then all answers will come to you. They have been waiting to serve you. Everything you have ever asked will be revealed to you. It works for me every time.

DRUGS

Those who are addicted to drugs like heroin love the good feeling when the compulsive thinking mind (Ego) no longer controls their being. They get a glimpse of ecstasy which is a high vibrational state that is beyond compulsive mental states. The difference between those on drugs and meditators is that one is dependent on costly substances outside themselves, the other enters states of wellbeing and bliss of their choice and anytime by true mastery (meditation).

Advanced meditators can reach the point where they enter different states of consciousness at will. Their happiness is no longer dependent on outer circumstances, only the "captain" within, the mastery within. Those who live consciously are in the last state of enlightenment. Mastery and wisdom increase as they enjoy their journey of creation. At the point of death, one dies consciously if one lives consciously. Life and death are a blessing to such beings. Those who know how to live joyfully, enjoy surfing the waves of duality, perceiving duality through the eyes of Source (oneness love and pure bliss), and die mindfully/consciously. What else can one ask for? Fear cannot control the master for the master knows that he is beyond fear, lives a fearless life and death. Life is a blessing with such organic beings who are unified with Source, the powerful royal origin, the prince and princess, the king and the queen. They are you, you are Source, your heritage is deathless, infinite, intelligent and divine. Enjoy the journey that you came to experience. Enjoy as Source, creation is the purpose of your life. Live on your own terms, a life of joy, bliss, wellbeing and happiness. Anything that is not aligned with pure joy, happiness, love, and wellbeing - you don't have to join in or focus your attention on because whichever you focus your attention to, becomes your reality at that moment.

You are a powerful creator, a life force, life energy. Energies are governed by the law of attraction. Attracting those of like vibration is the key to manifestation.

CONSCIOUSNESS - THE KNOWING MIND

The knowing mind itself has form. A formless form of pure knowing. Advanced meditators can "see" the difference between this Source, body vibrations, and mental states. The knowing mind knows body sensations and mental states. This knower is also known by the unnamable that is Source.

CREATOR AND THE GAME WE PLAY

Our root or true nature is already Source whether we know it or not. The only difference between the realized ones and others is the realized ones know that their root is already Nirvana. They live at ease and are fearless of death for they know where they came from and where they return to after death. Once we know that, life becomes a game that we can choose to play the way we want to. After enlightenment, one sees clearly and objectively how the universe and body/mind works. Only when we are free from the body/mind, we can use them the way we want. When we identify with them, we cannot see clearly how they work, nor are we able to use them as a master of body mind. Body mind uses us before enlightenment. After enlightenment we consciously use the body mind. The clarity state of Source is the infinite dimension of wisdom that arises. Something can only arise from something that is nothing. Something is the limitation of that something itself. The nothingness is the infinite. It is Source, our true origin. Align with that, gain wisdom (mastery), and use the body mind as creator. Enjoy the journey of conscious creation that we came forth to experience.

DIFFERENT DIMENSIONS OF REALITY

There are three dimensions, body/mind, spirit, and Nirvana.

Body/mind is the dimension of mental states, sensations, the bodily perceptions of eyes, ears, noses, tongue, etc. This dimension is the root of ego belief. Not knowing who we really are originally, one can only identify with dimensions of duality: good/bad, right/wrong, ugly/pretty, etc. Duality is a sense of ego (person) versus others. When there is any separation, there is bound to be conflict, competition, jealousy, etc.

However, I use a higher dimension called spirit, but the name is just a tool for communicating the true experience. This is the dimension of consciousness. Along my journey of meditation, I experience different dimensions beyond the body like seeing my breath form or staying in expanded consciousness where I can be anywhere in the Cosmos that I choose because everything in the universe is consciousness. I am limitless. I am united with the state of oneness energy, pure love and bliss. The state of pure consciousness is called Brahman, the highest state of consciousness in the universe. It is a love and bliss vibration. We can attain such state through meditation. I experienced it in my very first ten days of Goenka Vipassana retreat.

The third dimension is Nirvana or the absolute. This dimension is nameless, formless, it is the mother of pure consciousness, Brahman itself. It is the mother of all things including the subtlest OM sound and subatomic particles. When we can see subatomic particles and hear the OM sound, rest assured that we are in Source consciousness. Only something that has no form can perceive something that has form. Be aware of the mind in the beginning of your journey after you realize the Source dimension because the mind is very sneaky and can try to interpret the experience from time to time. However, when you are aligned with Source long enough and grounded enough in that dimension, you will have clarity of mental states and how they work. Source dimension knows everything. Whatever we practice, we get better at. There is no exception even on the path of enlightenment. Instead of practicing the ego as we have been, we now practice a new dimension of freedom and intelligence that we all have within.

YOUR NATURAL FREEDOM

Your natural freedom is always available, the origin of who you are, the Source. You are Source experiencing consciousness of body/mind inside and out. Source dimension can never be destroyed, killed, or taken away from you. Something that has no form cannot be killed. You are deathless; even when you leave your body and experience your soul level. Your soul is deathless for it connects with the oneness origin that is Source. Only the human dimension has fear of death because there is a solid body of flesh and blood. However, realizing your deathless dimension while being alive as a human is a blessing. You will live without fear, without being controlled by limitation of the body/mind dimension. You start aligning with your higher self or cosmic intelligence of knowing. It is also called oneness dimension because consciousness is the same in everyone. Once you align with this dimension, you connect with life at an intimate level. You feel, know, and love everything and everyone. The more in alignment with source that we are, the more we become one with the whole. Source is the origin of unconditional love and connectedness. You naturally live a wholesome life among others for you are no longer controlled by ego. After enlightenment, you live as Source experiencing consciousness and its creation. The creation is conscious with wisdom and love because one functions based on oneness intelligence, the dimension of Brahman. Only love, bliss, goodwill, and understanding exist because one is no longer separated from the whole. The one field of conscious is life energy.

THE PATH OF PURIFICATION

I spent about three years with this path in meditation centers in Myanmar. This path includes morality, concentration, and wisdom.

Morality is presented to help beginners conduct good actions because it leads to good results. In other words, good action attracts good results.

Samadhi or Concentration is to help one attain higher states of frequencies such as joy, tranquility, bliss, equanimity, etc. One can also attain Nirvana this way. I witnessed a friend experience Nirvana after attaining the highest state of concentration. When the mind reaches perfect equanimity (which is the state of pure consciousness itself), one can also experience the cessation of pure consciousness and experience Nirvana.

Wisdom is often realized during Vipassana training where meditators experience everything as it is in order to understand the nature of non-self. It is a fleeting phenomena (impermanence), because attachment to something constantly changing brings suffering. Nirvana itself is also called non-self. Nirvana is the end of all attachments and all sufferings once we realize our true source and align as that dimension. Everything that is delusion (accumulated limiting belief) will be transformed under the light of pure consciousness. Whichever we practice, we get better at it. Aligning with consciousness or source dimensions, one gains higher clarity and wisdom for a creative journey of creation.

THE LAW OF ATTRACTION OR CAUSE AND EFFECT

Law of attraction or cause and effect are one and the same. It is just different interpretations and translations throughout thousands of years.

It basically means whatever we put out to the universe, we attract back. Creators or masters are those who are in charge of their emotions, and intention. They use emotions and intentions wisely because through awareness and intelligence of non-self (Source) they see how the universe works and are able to live in accordance with the creation that serves the highest good for all. Nirvana is the highest bliss and the wise are those who align with and radiate that quality to the whole. The more they radiate such quality, the more they attract the best and highest blessings to themselves.

DIFFERENT TYPES OF RELATIONSHIPS

There are three different types of relationships: conditional, unconditional, and the mixture of both.

Conditional relationships are often formed when a person or both interact based on ego. They come together for some reason such as money, status, beauty, etc. There is nothing wrong with this relationship, however, the ego always has conflict within and therefore without. When one is so full of limiting ego beliefs, one lives a very restricted and contracted life. One lives based on memories or conclusions of the mind and not so much on the feeling or intuition of the moment. Often when original conditions are gone, the relationship is gone with it unless they grow together to the next levels of love.

The mixture of conditional and unconditional relationships is often found within family members. They love each other and forgive one another easily because of the sense of belonging such as MY daughter, MY father, MY son, MY sister, etc. Love is unconditional because there is a sense of mine in it, the person indeed loves what belongs to THEM (ego attachment).

Unconditional love is often found in twin-flame couples and those who are enlightened. Just like enlightened ones, twin-flame couples experience love in the highest frequency, the love of awakened ones. They attract one another after both have attained certain levels of realizations or enlightenment. In my case, when my twin-flame first met me, he experienced immense oneness vibration in his heart space. Since that day, we always miss each other, we've become each other's best triggers and best teachers. The triggers that are experienced in twin-flame relationships are for the higher purpose of healing and evolving. They have telepathy with each other. They love each other more than anyone else, like perfectly balanced two pieces of yin-yang. The merging of their Tantra (sexual intimacy) is the form of healing and ascending to higher levels of love and bliss. They are high frequency couples. I experienced cosmic consciousness at the point of orgasm with my soulmate. That is how I know Tantra is real. The enlightened ones live in a state of oneness consciousness, or the state of Source where they are one with the whole. Nirvana is the highest dimension. Frequencies such as love, joy, bliss, etc, are qualities of Nirvana. Enlightened ones naturally radiate these qualities in their life. That is why they are called blessed ones. Because they embody such qualities, they continue attracting similar vibrations that serve their highest good, the most blessed and blissful journey. All of us have a twin-flame, the key is to live in alignment, and we will attract our twin-flame that has the quality that is a match with us. Happy people attract happy people.

MORE ON THE TWO TYPES OF NIRVANA

I call them the alive nirvana and the absolute nirvana.

The alive nirvana is useful to life because it allows us to align with that dimension and experience life. This is seen often in Zen and non-dual traditions.

The absolute nirvana is found often in Vipassana traditions where one practices to experience Nirvana at the end of the path. Compared with Zen and non-dual traditions, Vippasana traditions often prefer to be in seclusion to practice and experience Nirvana in a sitting position. Having time to practice in seclusion is tremendously beneficial because it helped me to understand very clearly how the body mind works together. Experiencing absolute Nirvana in sitting is very powerful because it is a complete state of recharging the whole body/mind mechanism. This state allows me to dissolve all pain and suffering of the body prior to entering the absolute. I love the experience.

However, a combination of the two is best for today's society. I myself don't want to be in seclusion the rest of my life because I love to share truth with others who are ready to hear it. This is when Zen, or alive Nirvana, is tremendously beneficial.

The state of alive nirvana is so beautiful. There is a sense of freedom and connectedness with the whole, the journey of discovering higher wisdom, intelligence, bliss, and gratitude never ends. Zen living is a beautiful life where one is rooted as Source/Nirvana and spontaneously flow in life.

CHALLENGE IS THE WISE'S BEST FRIEND

How do we recognize and appreciate something good if there is not an opposite to compare it with? Challenges are indeed opportunities for our growth to higher intelligence, creativity, and happiness. Challenge is a perfect opportunity to learn and advance our mastery, an opportunity for higher expansion. Life is always in the process of changing or in other terms, life is new and fresh every moment. Living in the memory of the past is living against nature, that is why one suffers. The only thing that is different from dead is alive. When we are alive, we experience the best of it. Be creative, participate in the fun, the joy, the life that is worth experiencing. Your root is already Nirvana, after death you return back to spirit and Nirvana, what do you have to lose? Fear itself is hell. Fear is a very low frequency based on the chart of Dr. David Hawkins. Don't let the limitation of others including religions be your limitation. Nirvana is infinite, it has no limit or boundary. Nirvana is the ultimate freedom. Anything that creates duality of fear or bondages is not the dimension of the ultimate truth.

FREQUENCY CONNECTION

My first master pointed me to the Om sound, and step by step, within 1.5 months, she used real quantum physics to move my consciousness out of my body. When I opened my eyes, I saw subatomic particles. The time came when I had to go back home. I thought my peace was unshakable. However, after a few days, I started being shaken by circumstances, irritable feelings I did not like. My master then told me it will take me another four years to attain full realization. A few days after that, another master who can see my aura and Akashic record also told me the same thing, that I would reach maturity of realization in four years. Two years later, another monk in Myanmar told me that it will take me another two years.

These masters are those who have access to Akashic records, that is how they saw beyond time-space and gave me an accurate answer. As I am sitting here writing, four years have passed and I can tell you, their predictions came true.

During those four years, I could not do anything in the world. I lost interest in everything in the duality world where most people function based on ego. I traveled a few times to southeast Asia for meditation with different groups and masters. Two of those years, I lived in forest meditation centers as a nun with determination to realize Nirvana in this very life and I did. After more challenges and realizations, bliss increased higher and higher until Nirvana was experienced, the cessation of consciousness. Time and space disappeared. I was not told about my level of attainment directly by my master in the forest retreat, he only suggested that I become a meditation teacher and that he would train me. He also asked me to give a Dhamma talk in front of the sangha (group of monks and nuns) and hundreds of meditators right after he finished his last Dhamma talk in a seven-day retreat. All my questions were answered because my experiences were in alignment with it. A 90 years old female teacher in U Ba Khin Meditation Center in Myanmar, classmate of Master Goenka told me that my experience was indeed Nirvana itself. At first I loved being in Absolute state while sitting and wanted to stay there forever. The dense, heavy vibrations of duality were unacceptable. I sensed it very clearly in my heart space.

At that time, I finished the book The Power of Now by Eckhart Tolle. I was in alignment with the Zen life style and attracted to Mooji Papa's teaching which allowed me to be rooted in Nirvana while spontaneously flowing in life. Though I still sense vibrations of duality around me, mastery just gets better and better. I know where I should be and where I should go. When I have to be in environments that are not so loving or nourishing, I know where to direct my consciousness that brings me ease, balance, and happiness. Life is fun, the path of discovery is beautiful.

THE NOBLE ONES

Through Vipassana training, I directly experienced different stages of enlightenment. There are four levels, the last state is Arahant. I realized that "Alive Nirvana" is key to fully living a human experience. Once the human dimension ceases and we die, we go back to spirit and connect with the Nirvana that we are. Nirvana is our origin, how can we even escape from it? We are deathless and infinite. The two traditions of meditation, purification and Zen are indeed mutually supportive paths for we humans. They lead to the discovery of connectedness with pure life force. The path then becomes fun and adventurous.

"Nirvana is the cessation of all sufferings" - Buddha.

Before enlightenment or the realization of Nirvana, life is suffering because of mental and physical attachments. Alive nirvana and absolute nirvana ends all suffering. Living in the Source has no attachment, nothing to suffer from. Source just experiences creation itself. The power of enlightened humans is creativity. The power to create reality that is according to the wisdom of the universe and the law of attraction (cause and effect). The perfect purity and well-being of the Absolute purifies everything. Who you really are cannot get sick, cannot die, cannot hate, and cannot suffer.

FEAR OF DEATH

We fear death when we don't know who we are at our core. Once we recognized it, fear of death vanishes because we know who we were before birth and where we return to after death. There is no fixed formula for where we return to after death. As we briefly discussed before, we are multi-dimensional with three bodies. Human body, energy body (spirit), and Nirvana. In my experience, when my body consciousness vanished, I became pure energy. When pure energy vanished I became pure knowingness. When pure knowingness vanished, I was the Absolute (Nirvana) itself. We are the necessary pieces/elements of universal intelligence experiencing its infinite creation. Just consciously enjoying your creation is the key. When you are conscious, you cannot go wrong. Consciousness itself is pure energy of love and connectedness. Only when we are so rooted in mental states (ego), can we behave badly to others. You can learn alignment through different paths of practice such as meditation, yoga, tai chi, dancing, singing, etc. Once you are conscious, everything is meditation, everything is the dance of creation, the dance of pure positive energy.

MANIFESTATION

This is the path of the brave because one lets go of ego and unites with the higher dimensions of reality, love and connectedness. This dimension is vast, open hearted and opposed to contracted energy of ego/attachments.

Manifestation on this path is effortless, we do what we are inspired to do based on the needs of collective energy. When we do what we love and are passionate about, the outcome carries that energy and radiates it to the whole and attracts similar vibrations of happiness and joy. Whichever vibrations that belong to happiness and joy including abundance, love, wellbeing, and higher levels of realization/enlightenment.

ENLIGHTENMENT AND WORK

After enlightenment, your new energy will take you to places and people who are aligned with who you became. It is the law of vibration, also known as the law of attraction or cause and effect. When you meet certain groups or are in environments that are heavy with the density of ego, you won't resonate. You will know exactly their current spirituality state. You can help them if they are open to help. Otherwise, you may chose to spend most of your time in environments that are aligned with who you are. Perhaps you spend more time alone with inspiration for creation. Everything that flows from you in such states is pure wisdom, love, and connectedness. Introvert or extrovert are just the terms that duality uses to label different states of a person. No one is in the same state all their life. I was asked by a millionaire executive years ago in the interview, "are you an introvert or an extrovert?" I replied without thinking "both, at times I enjoy being alone, at times I enjoy being with others that are aligned with the high vibrations of who I am". The wise live aligned with the highest frequencies of the universe. We cannot give what we don't have, we can only overflow what we are so full of. Only when we are so happy, so nourished, can we overflow that quality to others who come into our presence.

HOW WE DO, MATTERS

It is not what we do but how we do it that matters. Masters are those who make wise choices. Their actions are inspired by alignment. Only when they are in alignment, can they offer any inspiration. I was inspired by my mentor, master, and CEO many years ago, noticing that every step he took, he made sure it was safe. Slow is ok, but safe is very important. There is a saying that whatever the Zen master (enlightened one) does is always correct, because it comes from a state of freedom and consciousness. They think from the space of Source. The mind also thinks but in terms of old/past memories. Taking small safe steps is like building a house on a strong, stable foundation.

There are many ways we can express love and greatness in the world especially with today's technology. We can inspire many, create abundance, etc. without having to travel and meet people in person. I find myself when I am in my own energy field or in the pure vibrations of nature, I can really do and be my best. Creative actions arise and overflow as a result of my books and YouTube programs. There is beauty and art in a life of joy and connectedness. My path just gets more blissful everyday, as does my gratitude and appreciation for life and all of you.

IN CHARGE OF YOUR REALITY

When we don't take charge of our happiness and mastery, the ego inside and outside will.

When we give attention or importance to anything, it becomes our reality at that moment. This is very clear in the mind of an advanced meditator. Understanding the universal law of attraction (cause and effect), creators consciously choose to focus their minds on the highest frequencies possible. We call them the wise because they choose to live joyfully regardless of circumstances. Even when someone behaves negatively, the wise, through their aligned state and pure perception, see the beauty in it. That is seeing through the eyes of God (Source).

There are different levels of alignment. The law of the universe is such that the more we practice something, the better at it we get. The path of enlightenment is no exception. When you practice being rooted in Source, you stay there more frequently until it becomes automatic. There were times in my journey where consciousness was like a camera, seeing everything in one shot. I could see myself sitting, talking, laughing spontaneously with friends while "the camera " kept on witnessing. That dimension of consciousness has intelligence of Source. It understands interaction beyond human perception. Wisdom keeps on growing naturally once this dimension becomes automatic because it is the origin of all. There is no hate nor love, there is just pure knowingness and understanding from a state of connectedness. There is pure joy and happiness in anything that I do. People around me notice that clearly. Unconditional love is best quality to describe this state. Pure acceptance and radiation of joy is automatic in this state of awareness. I was drawn to places and met people who were so loving, wise, and happy like I am, we are drawn to each other like a magnet.

IT IS NOT ABOUT WORKING HARD

Either we allow intelligence to work for us and experience a life of joyful creation or we are stressed pursuing what we think is good. When we are in the state of goodness, the law of the universe unfolds goodness in our experiences. Life does not have any formulas, it is neither about surrendering nor being active, both are impermanent. We are life. Life is always in the process of becoming, it is ever new at every moment. When we align with Source, our actions at every moment are spontaneous. At times we may be more or less active but always inspired by wellbeing and wisdom. Happy people take happy actions.

QUANTUM PHYSICS AND SYNCHRONICITY

Even if we don't know something it does not mean that it doesn't exist. Scientists are discovering more and more things that enlightened people knew thousands of years ago. The more I walk this path as Source, the more I discover this infinite mystery of life. My energy automatically takes me to the people and information that are aligned with my energy. It is so clear in my experience that people from different parts of the world, though not knowing each other, can receive the same information at the same time via universal intelligence. This is quantum physics. There are people who communicate with me quantumly sending me thoughts and receiving mine. My twin-flame has this ability. One time he joined me in my sleep and we had intimate sex together. We have telepathy. That night I sensed his energy field, the light of intimate sex and orgasm. To scientists and the modern man this may be nonsence. I can convince my twin-flame to work with science if they want to discover the truth about consciousness and quantum physics. My twin-flame is already free from birth and death, he can die consciously or choose to prolong his life as he chooses. It is true mastery. He completely mastered his body/mind. Yoga Nanda is also one of the few with this ability, free from the body mind and can choose to let the body die anytime he wants.

THE POWER OF GROUP MEDITATION

As we discussed in earlier chapters, the Maharishi effect sends groups of meditators to places that have high crime and violence rates. They found that when the population of meditators rises to 1%, it reduce crime and violence on average 16%.

Meditation is not just about sitting, it is a state of alignment with one's true nature. That way it is easy for humans in today's society. However, for beginners, it is important to be in supportive environments where people also live in this state of awareness because it will more easily facilitate your alignment. Whether you know it or not, we all can sense thoughts and energies of those around us. For beginners, since the mental state (ego) is still strong, it is easy to be influenced by turbulent environments. The nature of the mind is such that, only when it sees the benefits of meditation will it be willing to surrender to the process. That is why I see many people give up on meditation because they lack clarity as to how energy works. Everything in the body/mind is energy and is constantly in connection with energy of the universe at the deepest level. All is one. The wise are those who are connected to and flow through life with it. They live with ease, their actions aligned with universal purpose which is the most beneficial for the whole. Words of wisdom that flow from this state of connectedness with source have true power of transformation. Many times, through my YouTube and books people feel connected with the flow of energy, and feel happy. Many of them feel the pure vibration of energy running through their physical body. They feel joy and bliss. Books that flow from Source or the now are not designed for intellectualizing or the thinking mind, but from a dimension beyond it, the dimension of pure flow of energy. It is the dimension of truth itself and the truth sets you free. Just allow the flow of truth to purify the limitations of the mind and allows the flow of connectedness in you. The more you are connected with such frequency, the more you are adept in wisdom and realize the inner teacher within, the source intelligence. When the books or talks that get you to this state of knowing and alignment of flow, you are in meditation. The more people reaching this level the more the frequency of humanity shifts to higher levels of wisdom, intelligent, unconditional love, and joy.

WALKING MEDITATION

When you walk, just allow the flow of movement as a watcher outside of the body. Over time you will enjoy the body walking. Consciousness becomes more and more natural and spontaneous. Freedom and joy become dominant.

Consciousness is everywhere, it can be inside or outside. Put your hand on your chest, can you feel your heartbeat?

It means that you can feel inside the body. Advanced meditators including myself, can feel any part of the body, at cellular level.

Open your eyes, can you see the environment around you?

Close your eyes, can you hear sounds around you?

Touch the floor, can you feel the coolness or warmth?

We can perceive the world not just inside the body but also outside. Consciousness is everywhere. The knowledge is everywhere.

Now close your eyes and observe the whole body from the outside in one shot. Can you "see" or "feel" the person that you normally call "me, myself" from outside? Is it really you?

There may be some thoughts that arise at this moment, be aware of them as well. Are those thoughts you?

Now, go beyond and observe from the outside the whole house you are in.

Can you see that your consciousness is also there?

It is a different level of perception, it is not physical but rather a spiritual dimension. Those who see the formless form can be anywhere in the universe that they want. Even now your consciousness can be on the moon or among the stars. It is the same particle that makes up the whole universe. Consciousness is infinite and limitless. You are everything and everywhere.

That which knows everything everywhere is Source. SOURCE IS THE FORMLESS THAT KNOWS EVEN THE KNOWER.

You cannot find Source because YOU ARE IT. You know everything, beyond time and space and are formless. Nirvana of infinite possibility, at this dimension, creates a life that you want to experience because knowledge and secrets of the universe just keep on unfolding on your path. Everything starts with thoughts and ends with enlightenment. Buddha, Christ, and Mother Teresa were all conscious creators, living a life based on wisdom, freedom and universal intelligence. They always radiated the highest qualities of existence. That is key to mastering the law of attraction for a beautiful life of meaning and fulfillment.

I love you! May you all realize your freedom in this very life and enjoy your path of creation.

Tammie.

Resources:

(1) Parnia, Dr. Sam. "OZ Talk: DR. Sam Parnia." , Doc-torOz, 31 March 2017,. https://youtu.be/tHcZc-JJEFw.

Nibbanic peace is the ultimate peace of Nirvana.

(2) https://www.bcgom/publications/2018/unleashing-power-of-mindfulness-in-corporations.aspx

(3) https://appleofperceptionlogspot.com/2019/03/chart-of-consciousnesstml

(4) https://www.academiadu/4010689/Consciousness

(5) Master Goenka: is the Founder of dhammarg. The organization have hundreds Centers around the world.

(6) Getting into The Vortex - Page 4- Paragraph 2

(7) The Physics of Spirituality, Mindvalley Talks, https://youtu.be/gj5zRx7G_cs

(8) Dr. Masaru Emoto and Water Consciousness : https://thewellnessenterprise.com/emoto/

(9) Maharishi Effect : https://maharishi-programmeslobalgoodnews.com/maharishi-effect/